Marketing & Operating A

PROFITABLE
HOME
INSPECTION BUSINESS

2nd Edition

Kevin O'Malley

AHIT | AMERICAN HOME INSPECTORS TRAINING
An Mbition Company

Marketing & Operating a Profitable Home Inspection Business, 2nd Edition

Product Manager: Chris Chirafisi

Executive Editor: Sara Glassmeyer

Subject Matter Expert: Kevin O'Malley

Project Manager: Arlin Kauffman, LEAP Publishing Services

Product Specialist: Abby Franklin

Director of Channel Marketing: Brad Tusing

Channel Marketing Manager: Jared Schulze

Cover Composition: Chris Dailey and Julianna Szamlewski

For product information and technology assistance, contact us at **American Home Inspectors Training Institute Sales Support, 1-800-441-9411.**

Library of Congress Control Number: 2015956656
ISBN-13: 978-1-62980-135-3
ISBN-10: 1-62980-135-6

American Home Inspectors Training
20225 Water Tower Blvd
Brookfield, WI 53045

Visit us at **www.ahit.com**

Printed in the United States of America
2 3 4 5 6 7 20

CONTENTS

Chapter Three

PHONE TRAINING PROGRAM

Chapter Four

THE OFFICE

Chapter Five

OPERATIONAL BUSINESS ACTIVITIES

Chapter Six

HIRING AND MANAGING EMPLOYEES

Chapter Seven

WEBSITES, ELECTRONIC AND SOCIAL MEDIA MARKETING

Chapter Eight
THE INSPECTION PLAN

CHAPTER
01 | OVERVIEW

INTRODUCTION TO THE HOME INSPECTION BUSINESS

Tens of thousands of people make a satisfying living with their inspection business. Most inspectors spend a lifetime working on their knowledge and skills and developing an incredible referral base. This success can be and is repeated by new entrants to the inspection business each year.

Home Inspection Business Statistics

- 5 million homes were sold in 2014.

- More than 80% of those homes were inspected.

- Over 4 million home inspections were performed in 2014.

- If a home inspection fee averaged $350, the home inspection industry is worth $1.4 billion annually.

- Home inspectors can reasonably perform two or three inspections per day (depending on size, etc.).

- An inspection by a single inspector on a home with one story, with a slab foundation, and around 1,500 square feet will average approximately 2.5 hours to perform.

- Working five days a week and averaging two $350 inspections a day for 50 weeks a year, an inspector can generate $175,000 or more per year before expenses.

- The business of home inspection is to provide people with knowledge about the properties they are buying, selling or dwelling in.

- The majority of home inspections are performed for homebuyers after they make a purchase offer and before they close on the purchase of the home.

- Understanding the inner workings of the real estate transaction is one of the most important parts of creating a successful inspection business.

- The main reason the home inspection profession emerged and grew over the past 30 years is real estate disclosure.

- Disclosure in the real estate transaction has fueled home inspections and should be fully understood and embraced by inspectors.

At a meeting of a group of inspectors, the discussion of marketing came up. They were asked to share one thing they did in the past month that they could attribute to actually making their phone ring to create an inspection order.
These were their responses:

- Client relationship was stated four times

- Professional look

- Report Summary

- Education was stated two times

- Cleanliness

- Company motto

- Attention to detail

- Being a member of HON Professional Support (www.HONProfessional.com)

- Consistency

- They are a father-son team

- Giving more than expected

- Going beyond standards

- When they stopped by open houses, they had an ice chest filled with soda/ water they offered the house-sitting agents

- They are three generations of inspectors

- They gave gifts to agents

- They send recipes to their agent list

- Chamber of Commerce

- Visiting open houses was stated three times

- Being an association member

- Giving free memberships to "Total Home Support" (www.homeownersnetwork.com)

- Ad in yellow pages was stated two times

- Referral from past client

- They made a phone call to all their top agents just to touch base

- ASHI website

- Links from RE websites

- CREIA website

- InterNACHI website

- Got a referral from another inspector

- Belonging to the Better Business Bureau

- Word of mouth

- Blogging

- Using their designations on everything

- Attended a business networking meeting

- Sent an e-mail blast to their agent list

- Sent a weekly newsletter to agent

The list above contains many important parts of creating an inspection business. Every inspector should be doing such things as getting educated and building credentials. However, many items on the above list are not "direct actions" taken to make the phone ring and only the items in italics are actions that could directly create business immediately. The reason other items come to mind may be because the inspector does not have a specific business/marketing plan and may not really be doing things specifically designed to generate work. The inspector may be working in his or her business and joining an association, the Better Business Bureau, or the Chamber of Commerce, for example, but is not actively working a process/plan to generate inspection orders. Those who made direct phone calls, sent an email blast, or visited an open house are taking the action necessary to create more work immediately but may still be lacking a day-by-day plan to get more work. Check out all the business resources at www.score.org/resources /tab-a to find a sample business or marketing plan.

The next question asked of the group of inspectors was "What makes them different or special over their competition?" Or what is their unique sales position or USP? These were some of their responses:

- They offer their own inspection warranty free with each inspection

- 200% guaranty on all inspections

- Video of inspection (one uses a remote camera)

- Uses a drone to inspect roofs

- Instant report delivery on site

- Uses a mold-sniffing dog

- Gives Home Recall Alerts for appliances through Home Owners Network

- Two-person inspection team for faster work

- Three-person inspection team

- Gives a free membership to Home Owners Network (www.homeownersnetwork.com)

- Thermal imaging

- 203K inspection consulting

- Presale inspections (listing inspections for sellers)

- Uses Facebook

- Uses LinkedIn

- Uses Twitter

- Good at search engine optimization (SEO) (getting their websites to come up first on search engines)

- Teaches continuing education classes to agents

- Does many real estate office presentations

- Visits open houses every weekend

- Uses send out cards (a Web-based card sending service)

- Posts many inspection videos on YouTube.com

- Energy audits

- Writes inspection articles and gets published

- Annual maintenance inspections (every year for past clients)

- Does commercial inspections

- Specializes in old houses

- Specializes in first-time homebuyers

- Attends all RE Association events (sponsors as much as possible for exposure)

- Is a member of all Real Estate Boards in area and attends all meetings

That list provides many good ideas and many inspectors today can be great at marketing, however it is important to understand what makes you different from your competition and to promote that difference in all of your marketing efforts. It is consistency and planning that make the difference in the long run. You must create a business and marketing plan that will keep you on target, make your efforts consistent, and build your business.

Purpose of This Book

This guide will familiarize you with the home inspection business, setting up your office, creating a marketing plan, and beginning your business success path. There is nothing easy about it—you must be dedicated to your business, build your knowledge, and expand your marketing efforts.

Types of Inspection Services Currently Being Offered

The Buyer Inspection

The inspection bought and paid for by a buyer involved in a real estate transaction is the most common home inspection performed in the industry today. In your early months in business, you can expect 99% of your inspections to be buyer inspections. Later, you'll be able to make inroads with seller inspections and home checkup inspections, reducing the number of buyer inspections. But have no doubts about the buyer inspection—it's your primary service.

To your established referral base, buyers will come to you through your marketing efforts. Real estate agents, mortgage brokers, attorneys, and other people associated with the real estate transaction will suggest your inspection company as one of three or four home inspection companies.

When buyers call to ask about your services, your scheduler will be responsible for closing these sales on the phone. The *Home Maintenance Manual,* used as a gift for customers of the buyer inspection, was developed to help you secure the sale. Other unique selling propositions, USPs, will be discussed later in this book.

THE BUYER INSPECTION	
The Customer	The buyer in a real estate transaction, generally after making an offer on a property.
Customer's purpose	To get an honest and impartial report of the home's condition, to be informed of any problems and upcoming repairs, and to avoid unpleasant surprises after the sale.
Customer source	Referral.
Marketing	Ongoing meeting with, networking with, and promoting your services to real estate agents, lending institutions, attorneys, and other parties to the real estate transaction.
Closing the sale	Skilled, trained scheduler on the phone to capture the appointment. Also should be available on your website. Use of any of your company's USPs as an incentives to close.

The Seller Inspection

The seller inspection, commonly called the listing inspection, is a program you can enter into with a broker to lock in all the inspections for the sellers listed with that broker. The marketing thrust for seller inspections will be directed at potential brokers. This program can be advantageous to the broker.

Sometimes, you'll do inspections for sellers who come to you by referral, although it isn't common in the industry for the seller to purchase the inspection.

THE SELLER INSPECTION	
The Customer	The seller in a real estate transaction, generally before the property is shown. Can be paid for by the real estate broker in a listing program so the broker would then be your customer.
Customer's purpose	To be able to comply with full disclosure laws, to be informed of problems and repair them before showing, and to avoid lawsuits after a sale. In the case of the broker, to increase listings, attract buyers, and close the sale faster.
Customer source	Calls you after a referral. With a listing program, all the broker's sellers are locked in.
Marketing	Referral base marketing. Presenting the listing program to the broker and contracting to inspect all its listings.
Closing the sale	Skilled, trained scheduler on the phone to capture an appointment. Also should be available on your website. The sale is already closed if a listing program is in place.

The Review with Buyer Inspection

A review inspection is performed for the buyer in a transaction *after* an initial seller inspection has been done. The *same* inspector returns to the property for a walk-through to review the initial inspection with the buyer.

This type of inspection is tied to the seller inspection and can be a strong aspect of the listing program entered into with a broker. The advantage to the broker is being able to assure potential buyers of already-inspected properties that they can have the house re-inspected at a lower cost than if they bought a full inspection. If you can negotiate it, the broker may pay for the review inspection. But in most cases, the broker may only promote the idea to the buyer. The Home Maintenance Manual is used as a gift to help you capture this sale.

THE REVIEW WITH BUYER INSPECTION	
The Customer	The buyer, where the inspector performed the original inspection for the seller or the broker if they paid for the inspection.
Customer's purpose	To have the *Property Inspection Report* made available by the seller and verified by the inspector who performed the inspection and to have the inspector explain and show any defects and deficiencies noted in the report and update it if those repairs were completed. Keep in mind that if you bless a repair (say it is correct) that you take the responsibility for that repair. Best practice would be to note the repair and suggest that your client obtain the receipts for the repair so they know who to contact if anything goes wrong with the item after they move in.

Customer source	Arrangement with the seller or agent to contact the inspector when a buyer is found and to follow up.
Marketing	Including review inspections as an integral part of listing program with broker.
Closing the sale	Generally following up with the seller and agent, using the Home Maintenance Manual as an incentive. The sale already may be closed as part of listing program.

Radon Testing

Radon testing can be performed for buyers, sellers, and homeowners. Most often, you will be asked to perform radon testing for homebuyers, and this can be started during the home inspection. There are specific requirements for doing radon testing; training and special equipment is needed. Make sure you are well versed in all things radon before starting this service. Check your state's radon testing requirements as well.

RADON TESTING	
The Customer	The buyer, the seller, or the homeowner.
Customer's purpose	To check the property for the presence of high levels of radon.
Customer source	Home-buying clients can be upsold, home sellers can be upsold, and homeowners can be sold.
Marketing	Include radon testing services in your standard home inspection brochures, website, and office presentations. Can be sold on-site during a home inspection.
Closing the sale	Done on the phone during the home inspection order process or on your website with the order process.

Home Maintenance Inspection

This inspection is the service provided in the home checkup program. It's a standard home inspection performed for a homeowner who isn't involved in a real estate transaction. The home maintenance inspection is sold as a checkup inspection for homeowners who have an interest in keeping their homes in good condition and need professional help doing so.

This service is an innovative move in the industry. With the home checkup concept, you will be creating a broader market for home inspection products as well as continuing revenue from existing customers. This is rarely done by home inspectors. They are usually chasing the next person who is purchasing a home instead of trying to create programs that get them back in the homes of people they've already worked for. Getting people who used your service in the past and liked it/you to use your service again is far less expensive than continually looking for new customers. Your task is to come up with an appealing reason why people should have their homes inspected every year. You want to show them how you can help them take care of their homes and stay on top of maintenance, which in the long run saves them money, avoiding expensive problems.

Customers who join the Home Maintenance Plan are an important customer source for the home maintenance inspection. Mail and telemarketing campaigns to sell the maintenance inspection and the plan should become part of your continuing marketing efforts. Every client for whom you perform a home inspection becomes a target for this marketing. At the end of every home inspection, you should explain the value of this service and discuss how they can take advantage of having you come to their home once a year for a checkup. Here are some simple statistics to consider: If inspectors are performing 30 inspections a month for 10 months each year, they are doing 300 inspections a year. If inspectors are performing only presale home inspections, they will never have an inspection scheduled for next year because home inspections typically get booked within a week or two of the purchase offer. If those same inspectors were offering annual maintenance inspections and just 10% of their prepurchase clients booked with them each year, they would have prebooked 30 inspections a year in advance. After 10 years, that is conservatively 300 inspections prebooked for the following year. Obviously they may lose some because people move, but in those cases, wouldn't the homeowners want them to inspect their next home? Home inspectors do very little to market to past clients. This is a program that keeps you in front of your past clients and that you should be presenting to all your clients and on your website to visitors.

HOME MAINTENANCE INSPECTION	
The Customer	A homeowner not involved in a real estate transaction.
Customer's purpose	To learn what to do in the interest of keeping the home in optimum condition, to be informed of any repairs needed, and to learn how to avoid problems in the future. You could be on call to inspect repairs or upgrades done by the homeowner or contractors when needed. There are lots of reasons for you to be a regular part of a homeowner's life.
Customer source	Members of the Home Checkup Plan, previous customer lists, and the general public of homeowners.
Marketing	Mail, electronic, and telemarketing campaigns to previous customers and homeowners and reminders to Plan members.
Closing the sale	Applicable in telemarketing when sales are closed on the phone by a trained salesperson. Mail/email sales by return call or mail/email response. Also should be available on your website.

Home Maintenance Service Plan

The Plan is a key element in establishing an ongoing relationship with your customers and selling them additional inspections in the future. Under the Home Maintenance Plan, a member:

- Pays a nonrefundable initial fee for a five-year membership.

- Can purchase up to five home maintenance inspections during the five-year period but is not required to buy any.

- Pays an inspection price that's fixed over the five years they're in the plan.

- Are reminded annually about the next inspection.

The Home Maintenance Plan is a commitment to developing additional products for your existing customers.

HOME MAINTENANCE SERVICE PLAN	
The Customer	The buyer and previous customers.
Customer's purpose	To have the home inspected on a regular basis to keep the home in optimum condition, to be informed of any repairs needed, and to avoid future problems.
Customer source	Buyers at buyer and review inspections and previous customers.
Marketing	Introduction to buyers at an inspection and follow-up; mail and telemarketing promotions to previous customers.
Closing the sale	Inspectors at the inspection site, mail, and skilled telemarketing person on the phone. Also should be available on your website.

Commercial Inspections

The real estate market for commercial properties is an estimated $15 trillion. The commercial real estate market continues to move through the recovery phase of the economy, putting it in a strong position to grow. But even if it doesn't grow, it is so big that inspectors should not overlook it. This market offers a huge opportunity with much larger fees involved, but also comes with a new set of challenges. Commercial buildings have different systems compared with residences, making them more complex to inspect. Inspectors must have specialized training or approach commercial inspections very differently. Home inspections can typically be performed by one person inspecting everything. A commercial inspection has so many complex systems that it makes sense to work with a team of specialized contractors, hiring them to inspect systems such as three-phase electrical systems, complex HVAC systems, commercial roofing, and elevators. Now the inspector becomes the lead on a commercial inspection and uses other experts to perform a professional inspection. With a lack of standards for performing a commercial inspection, the work can take on many forms. However, some inspectors choose to follow *ASTM E2018-08, Standard Guide for Property Condition Assessments: Baseline Property Condition Assessment Process*, which offers guidelines for performing an overview examination of a structure. Commercial inspections can be very lucrative and challenging, which is something to consider if you want to expand your business in the future.

COMMERCIAL INSPECTIONS	
The Customer	Commercial property buyers can be individuals and investment groups.
Customer's purpose	To have the building inspected, to be informed of any needed repairs, and to avoid future problems. Most commercial buyers want the cost of repairs as well as information on the condition. A commercial buyer may also want a future maintenance plan with costs.
Customer source	Commercial real estate brokers are a good place to start in finding customers.
Marketing	Introduction to buyers by attorneys, commercial brokers, and investment groups.
Closing the sale	Inspectors may be required to write proposals for commercial inspections that include a defined scope of the work to be performed. Because each commercial building is unique, you may want to do a preinspection site visit so that you understand what is involved and can explain to your clients what the inspection will and will not cover. You should call or meet the client to get an understanding of the information they are looking for. They may not care about the roof but want to know the cost of maintaining the parking lot. Every commercial buyer is different, as is every building. You must be clear about your work and your client's expectations.

Mold Testing

Mold testing is becoming a typical option in the home inspection process. Many inspectors receive training per EPA guidelines and offer this service with their home inspections as an option. Mold testing requires specific equipment and can be an additional revenue stream for home inspectors.

MOLD TESTING	
The Customer	Homebuyers, sellers, and owners.
Customer's purpose	To determine the presence of mold and how to remediate it.
Customer source	Buyers at buyer inspections, seller inspections, and homeowners.
Marketing	Introduction to clients on website, during home inspection bookings, and during home inspections.
Closing the sale	Office staff and inspectors at the inspection site. Also should be available on your website.

Energy Audits

Energy audits help in determining how energy efficient a home is and ways to implement low-cost energy-saving solutions. You should understand energy management and areas of energy loss or high consumption and be able to create plans that help people save energy and ultimately money.

ENERGY AUDITS	
The Customer	Homebuyers, sellers, and owners.
Customer's purpose	To determine the energy efficiency of the home and know what to do to save energy and money.
Customer source	Buyers at buyers' inspections, seller inspections, and homeowners.
Marketing	Introduction to clients on website, during home inspection bookings, and during home inspections.
Closing the sale	Office staff and inspectors at the inspection site. Also should be available on your website.

In-Progress Construction Inspection

There is a call for private inspectors doing in-progress construction inspections on homes being built. They would serve as overseers of the progress of the construction from start to finish or during one or more disciplines such as installing the structural steel in the foundation or laying block walls. These jobs can be performed for the buyer of the new home, municipalities, contractors, and others. Usually paid at an hourly rate, they can be sold in blocks of time or visits. Making 10 or more visits to the house construction site during the building process is not unusual.

IN-PROGRESS CONSTRUCTION INSPECTION	
The Customer	Homebuyers, owners (during remodel), municipalities (contract labor), and contractors (to oversee or check on subcontract work).
Customer's purpose	To ensure the quality and timeliness of the construction work.
Customer source	New construction sites, homebuyers, municipalities, and builders.
Marketing	Introduction to clients on website and marketing to builders and municipalities.
Closing the sale	Office staff, sales visits to builders' offices, and online.

Condo Association Reserve Analysis

Working with condominium homeowner associations can be incredibly lucrative. Each year the homeowner association (HOA) board of directors must evaluate their common properties and determine what maintenance, repairs, and replacements need to be performed. A detailed budget and plan must be created, and inspections are typically needed. Home inspectors have the knowledge to do these inspections and to assist HOA boards with their annual requirements.

CONDO ASSOCIATION RESERVE ANALYSIS	
The Customer	Homeowner associations. Each association will have a board of directors that you would pitch this program to.
Customer's purpose	To determine annual maintenance, repairs, and budgets for the buildings and common areas. Many times, inspections of exterior walls, roofs, pool areas and anything common that the association maintains is needed.
Customer source	Homeowner association meetings.
Marketing	Introduction to clients on website. Proposals to HOA for annual assessment inspections and more.
Closing the sale	Office staff and inspectors at the HOA meetings.

Roof Certification and Inspection

Roof certifications are separate from a home inspection. Home inspectors typically do not issue roof certifications that guarantee the condition or integrity of the roof. Roof certifications can help sell homes and may be required by lenders or mortgage companies. The purpose of a roof certification is to inform a buyer about the condition of the roof, reveal its remaining life expectancy, and identify any needed repairs. Roof certifications can give buyers peace of mind knowing that the roof is serviceable for a certain number of years. The person issuing the certification usually requires certain repairs before he or she will issue the certificate and warranty. Roof certifications can be performed by home inspectors, roofing inspectors, or roofing specialists. To issue a certification that the roof is leak-free, the inspector will typically report on the condition of roofing materials, ridges, vent flashings, drip edges, drains, chimney flashing, and more. If any of these items are not in good condition, repairs will be required before the certification is issued. If the repairs are completed or no repairs were required, the roofing certification will include an estimate of the roof's remaining years of life and certify its inspection. A certification is typically a warranty against problems on the roof for a specific period of time (for example, two to five years). The issuer of the certificate is responsible if any leaks occur and would do the necessary repairs. More information and certification can be had at: www.nrcia.org

ROOF CERTIFICATION AND INSPECTION	
The Customer	Homebuyers, sellers, lenders, agents and owners.
Customer's purpose	To determine whether a roof is watertight and possibly how long a roof will last. To purchase a repair warranty on the roof. Sellers use certifications to give assurances to a buyer. The provider of the roofing certification is typically on the hook for leaks for a stated period of time.
Customer source	Buyers at buyer inspections, seller inspections, and homeowners.
Marketing	Introduction to clients on website, during home inspection booking, and during home inspections.
Closing the sale	Office staff, inspectors at the inspection site and online.

Pest Inspection

Pest inspection is different than pest control. That being said, there are strict state and federal regulations pertaining to pest control in most areas, although there are not as many regulations dealing with the inspection for pests. However, before starting this area of business, it is wise to do your homework and check your state's requirements for doing pest inspections. Some inspectors do pest inspections as part of their home inspection process. Others do separate inspections and issue separate reports. There are even a few inspectors who own and operate pest control companies. All of these are options if they are done according to each state's rules and laws.

PEST INSPECTION	
The Customer	Homebuyers, sellers, and owners.
Customer's purpose	To determine the presence of pests and how to remediate them.
Customer source	Buyers at buyer inspections, seller inspections, and homeowners.
Marketing	Introduction to clients on website, during home inspection booking, and during home inspections.
Closing the sale	Office staff, inspectors at the inspection site, and online.

Permit Research

Are there permits for the home and other structures on the property? A home inspection will not make this determination. It may turn up evidence that leads you to believe that something might not be permitted, but you will never know for sure without checking with the local building authority. Why would anyone want to know this? If a structure was not permitted, it was built illegally. If it was not inspected during construction, it could be unsafe or a hazard. If the building authority wants it removed, that can happen. So doing permit research prior to purchasing any structure is important. It is an easy job but one that gets overlooked by many buyers and agents. For a fee, home inspectors can do the permit research and provide this information to buyers, sellers, and real estate agents.

PERMIT RESEARCH	
The Customer	Homebuyers, sellers, agents, lenders, attorneys and owners.
Customer's purpose	To determine whether the structure is permitted legally.
Customer source	Buyers at buyer inspections, seller inspections, and homeowners.
Marketing	Introduction to clients on website, during home inspection booking, and during home inspections.
Closing the sale	Office staff, inspectors at the inspection site, and online.

Expert Testimony

Determining who is right and who is wrong can make for a profitable business. An expert witness provides opinions on situations under disagreement or determines what happened in a disaster, for example.. Expert testimony or witness work is a specialty that many inspectors gravitate toward after they have had a good deal of inspection experience. Some experts are specialists in one field, such as HVAC installations or roofing, and they limit their expert work to those fields only. Any expert witness gets paid to research, inspect, discover, uncover, and provide opinions on many things. Providing expert testimony is a fascinating area of work that provides a lucrative income.

EXPERT TESTIMONY	
The Customer	Homebuyers, sellers, real estate agents, attorneys, builders.
Customer's purpose	To determine the causes of issues, costs of repairs, and results of tests.
Customer source	Attorneys, real estate agents, and builders.
Marketing	Introduction to clients on website, visits to attorneys' offices, known as the expert in your area.
Closing the sale	Creating a curricula vitae, or CV, and sending it to construction defect attorneys.

203K Inspections and Consulting

203K inspections are a great way to become more than just a home inspector. This government loan program assists buyers who want to purchase run-down properties and get financing and assistance necessary to fix up the property and then have a full mortgage available to them when they move in. Home inspectors can become 203K consultants and assist buyers with continuing construction inspections and consulting. Getting on the approved FHA 203K consultants list is critical, as is learning to work with all the forms and inspection processes.

203K INSPECTIONS AND CONSULTING	
The Customer	Homebuyers, investors, and agents.
Customer's purpose	To determine the issues with bringing a home up to standards, figure costs for repairs, and do inspections during construction.
Customer source	Buyers for rundown housing and investors in fixer-uppers.
Marketing	Introduction to clients on website.
Closing the sale	Office staff and online.

THE REAL ESTATE INDUSTRY

The industry is made up of independent real estate firms and franchised real estate firms. Of these firms, we define them according to the number of agents working for the firm as follows:

- Small: fewer than 5 agents

- Medium: 5 to 20 agents

- Large: more than 20 agents

The largest real estate firms can have 200 or more agents. The old rule in the industry used to be that 20% of the firms did 80% of the business. Today the number is closer to 10% of the real estate firms conducting 90% of the business. The biggest and the best have gotten bigger and better. The leaders in any community will most likely be franchised real estate companies such as Coldwell Banker, RE/MAX, Keller Williams, ERA, Sotheby's, Corcoran, Better Homes and Gardens, and Berkshire Hathaway. Even Zillow is venturing into brokerage since online searches became the norm for finding homes.

The Players

There are two main categories of people in the real estate business—the real estate broker-owner and the real estate agent. About 58% are women according to the National Association of REALTORS®. The term *real estate agent* refers to both brokers and agents, however an agent may not yet be a broker.

A person who wants to enter this industry must study and take exams to become a licensed real estate agent with the state. After meeting requirements by working as an agent for a given number of years, an agent can take the broker exam and become a licensed broker. Three certifications can be earned:

- GRI: A graduate of the real estate institute

- CRS: A certified residential specialist

- CRB: Certified Real Estate Brokerage Manager

Brokers and agents can be members of a professional organization called the National Association of REALTORS® (NAR). The organization has a Board of Realtors for each state in each local area. The local Board of Realtors holds meetings on a regular basis to present topics that are important in the industry and hosts social gatherings. Most of the big real estate firms belong to the NAR and its local boards.

NOTE: The Board of REALTORS® offers an affiliate membership to business people involved in the real estate process, such as home inspection companies, lending institutions, attorneys, appraisers, and title companies. Joining the local Board of REALTORS® allows you to stay up to date on Realtor issues and to socialize with brokers, agents, and other types of affiliates. This is part of the networking process required to build a strong referral base.

Roles shift in the real estate industry depending on who lists a property for sale and who brings the buyer to the property. Co-broker relationships allow an agent working for one broker to find buyers of properties listed with other brokers. These same co-broker relationships mean that *all* agents working for these brokers represent *sellers*, not buyers.

Here are some terms that will help you sort out the roles.

- Listing broker. This is the real estate company that has signed the listing contract with the seller. The listing broker lists and promotes the sale of the property.

- Listing agent. This is the agent who represents the seller of a property listed with its broker. The agent works with the seller to prepare the property for showing, holds open houses, generally promotes the property, and looks for buyers.

- Selling broker. This is the real estate company whose agent finds a buyer for the property listed with the listing broker.

- Selling agent. This is the agent who brings the buyer to the sale. It would seem that the selling agent represents the buyer, but that is not so. Due to the co-broker relationship, this agent represents the seller and must disclose to the seller anything the buyer reveals, including how high the buyer would go on the offer.

- Buyer broker. In the last seven to nine years in some parts of the country, a new figure has appeared. This is the buyer broker who truly represents the buyer in a real estate transaction, who works only for the buyer, and who holds everything the buyer reveals in confidence. Agents tend not to like them.

The listing broker is also the selling broker if the real estate company both lists a seller property and finds a buyer for the property. Likewise, the listing agent is also the selling agent if he or she is showing the property and finds a buyer. An agent can be acting as a listing agent for his or her broker and finding a buyer for another broker's property, so he or she would be a listing agent and a selling agent at the same time.

How the Money Works

The seller of a property pays a commission when the property is sold. That commission is commonly 6% of the sales price of the home, but it can go as high as 8% in some parts of the country. This chart shows how the commission is normally divided up, where 100% represents the full commission amount paid on a sale.

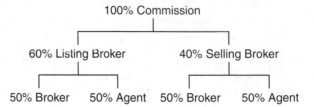

Here's an example to show how it works. Suppose a property sells for $200,000 and the commission is 6%.

The example shows how commissions are commonly handled. Agents who are touted as selling $1,000,000 worth of property may only have made $15,000 in total on those sales ($1,000,000 × 6% commission × 50% average broker take × 50% broker/agent split). But there can be variations on the broker/agent split. Often, the top performing agents will negotiate a higher percentage with the broker and may earn as much as a 75% cut of the broker's commission.

RE/MAX, Realty Executives, and other companies offer an exception to the rule and have a different kind of relationship with its agents. RE/MAX agents earn 100% of the commission normally split between the broker and the agent. Agents pay a monthly service charge to the RE/MAX broker for the right to be a RE/MAX agent. The broker earns the monthly charge whether or not the agent has earned any commission.

The Documents

You should study the set of standardized paperwork that is associated with a real estate transaction. Get samples from a helpful real estate agent. Some of them are available for sale-by-owner situations at an office supply store.

- **Listing contract** between broker and seller stating the term of listing and commission percentage.

- **Property disclosure report** that the seller fills in to disclose information about the property (mandatory in some states).

- **Property disclosure form** that the selling agent is required to give to the buyer stating that the agent is working for the seller.

- Transfer Disclosure Statement or TDS is another name for these forms

- **Offer to purchase form** in addition to the **amendments** and **addendums** that are eventually added to turn it into a contract. These usually include the home inspection contingency.

The Transactions

The following steps are common to the real estate transaction process.

1. An agent gets the listing with the seller. The listing contract is negotiated at this time. The seller generally wants a short term of three months so that he or she can switch agents if the house doesn't sell. The listing agent wants a long term of six months or more so that there is time to sell the house. The commission percentage may be negotiated as well. Sometimes,

sellers know what percentage is standard in the community and won't negotiate, but agents will try to up the percentage if they can.

The listing agent will conduct a market analysis to set the price of the house by studying selling prices of comparable homes sold in the area within the last year.

2. The seller fills out the property disclosure report. Sellers are required to disclose to prospective buyers everything they know about their home. The seller signs this form, but the listing agent participates in the process. Included in this step, the agent/broker is required to inspect the property he or she is listing and disclose anything that might affect the value or desirability of the property. This is the step that raises liability potential for the agent and the listing broker and the reason home inspections grew in popularity and use. Many people believe that the inspection relieves some of the liability of disclosure when in fact it does not. If either the seller or broker knows something about the property, he or she is supposed to disclose it to all prospective buyers.

3. The house is put on the market. The listing agent puts the house in the multiple listing service (MLS). Licensed agents reference this service that details properties for sale by price and use it as a marketing tool with buyers. The agent also advertises the property, holds open houses, and tries to find a buyer.

4. Buyers view the house. Buyers can come on their own to open houses, in which case interested buyers are quickly scooped up by the listing agent. However, two agents, listing and selling, are part of 90% of real estate transactions. That means it's far more common for a selling agent to bring a buyer to a property than for the listing agent to find a buyer. And that means that listing agents work with selling agents to bring the deal to a close.

5. An offer to purchase is made. The selling agent helps the buyer write an offer to purchase the house, and the listing agent helps the seller with counteroffers. The parties go through this stage of negotiating and settling on the price. Parties go through the contingency phase. The seller and the buyer negotiate contingencies to the offer to purchase. Common examples are:

   • Financing contingency. The deal depends on whether financing can be arranged. Some buyers go to the bank first for preapproval on a mortgage amount. Others will need post-approval for the mortgage amount after the offer is made.

   • Home sale contingency. The offer is contingent on the sale of the buyer's current home.

   • Home inspection contingency. The offer depends on the findings from a home inspection. One of these clauses could be used:

— The buyer can back out of the deal if he or she is not satisfied with the findings of the home inspection.

— The seller's right to cure clause, which the seller wants, stating that the seller has the right to cure the problem or negotiate a resolution to the problem if a deficiency is found during the home inspection.

6. If contingencies are met, the deal closes. About 10% of real estate deals fall through because of *any or all* of the contingencies. About 7.5% fall through because of the home inspection. In other words, about 75% of all deals that fall through after an offer is accepted are because of the home inspection. That should put into perspective the effect the home inspection can have on the transaction and provide some insight into how the agent feels about the home inspection.

The Real Estate Agent/Broker Relationship

To earn their income, agents rely on the real estate transaction closing. Their commission is at stake, and for obvious reasons, they don't want any deals to fall through. They are aware that the findings from a home inspection can be a deal breaker.

Typically, the agent present with the buyer at a home inspection is the selling agent; however, many buyers' agents also attend the inspection. Remember, the selling agent can also be the listing agent for the property, but usually, two agents are involved with the transaction.

An agent should prepare the buyer about the condition of the house and is present for the home inspection. An agent should be aware of the general condition of the house and know that some deficiencies will be reported at the home inspection. Some agents may avoid the fact that anything is wrong with the house, but the home inspection will bring those deficiencies to light.

Agents are in full work mode with each transaction and could be experiencing one or more of the following:

- Seeing the inspection as an obstacle standing between the agent and the deal.

- "Holding their breath" during an inspection, hoping nothing is found.

- Feeling nervous and worried.

- Being surprised over major problems uncovered in an inspection.

If there are buyer brokers in your area, instead of a selling agent, one may be present with the buyer at a home inspection. The buyer broker, who truly represents the buyer and has his or her interests in mind, will be less nervous about the inspection.

Home inspection is not an easy profession because of this natural tension the real estate agent feels toward the inspector and the perception the agent may have that you're working on opposite sides. Here's some general advice about dealing with real estate agents:

1. Help the real estate agents to understand that your work can protect them with regard to liability. The role of an impartial third-party inspection can aid in the issue of disclosure responsibility and potentially lessen liability for everyone.

   You play a positive role in their business. When real estate agents focus on this larger picture of how you help them and not focus on the outcome of each deal, you've accomplished a great deal in the relationship.

2. Be professional when dealing with real estate agents. You have an ethical duty to report any findings from your client's home inspection. You should not let anyone influence your findings in any way.

3. Sometimes, you will lose real estate agents who become upset when the deal doesn't close (for example, when a home has major issues). (The majority want their clients to have a problem-free home.) Even the best agents can get upset when you find something wrong and the deal falls through. Most take the proper perspective and are able to handle it, but others may hold it against you.

   One measure you can take to prevent this from happening is to call the agent after an inspection for a communications check. That is, make sure that what you said (or meant to say) at the inspection was correctly communicated to the agent. It's possible that the agent misunderstood something you said and has a distorted view of the inspection. Any bad feelings or overreactions the agent may have about the inspection can be dissipated with a friendly chat.

4. Keep the real estate agent in mind when you're handling complaint calls. At times, you may want to offer a settlement on a complaint, even when it isn't necessary, to save the agent also named in the case. Doing so creates goodwill in that relationship.

5. Your best approach is to be up front with agents—always. Be clear about what you can and cannot do as well as what you will and will not do. Communicate findings directly, precisely, and honestly. Sometimes, the buyer does not want the agent present at an inspection and will ask you to keep the contents of the inspection report confidential. Always honor that request and be direct with the agent who tries to get information from you, reminding him or her that you cannot legally do that.

Honesty and integrity is the best approach. The reputation of your home inspection company is at stake. And in home inspection, a good reputation *is* your business.

Follow *AHIT's* **marketing approach.** Marketing to real estate agents with ongoing meetings with, promotions for, and presentations to agents and attending

Board of Realtor functions will contribute to a growing and positive relationship with the community of real estate agents.

After reading about the dangers in the relationship with agents, it should be obvious how a **listing program** arrangement with a broker can turn that relationship upside down. When a broker enters into an agreement with you to provide inspections for his or her listings *before* they're shown, you're no longer a deal breaker to the broker. Now you're someone who is improving the broker's chances of attracting buyers, reducing the number of deals that fall through, and closing deals faster. Suddenly you're on the same side.

CHAPTER
02

ESTABLISHING YOUR BUSINESS

INTRODUCTION

Business does not just start itself. You need to create a plan and work it. Just as you were trained to perform inspections, you might consider taking some courses for business planning. Consider your local community college or the Web for some simple business planning courses. At least spend time putting together a business plan. Get help with business planning from SCORE, the Service Corps of Retired Executives, which was mentioned in Chapter 1. SCORE also provides assistance at numerous offices across the nation by providing you with a business mentor. Check out www.score.org. Another useful resource for starting your own business is the U.S. Small Business Administration: www.sba.gov/writing-business-plan.

PURPOSE OF THE BUSINESS PLAN

The goal of your business plan is to create a roadmap to your success. It helps you identify your specific marketplace, the competition, service costs, business needs, marketing plans, and much more. If you ask for a business start-up loan from your bank, it will require a business plan from you. But most importantly, your business plan will be a living document that you use to start and operate your inspection business—a very important document to say the least. These are the key questions a business plan answers:

- What is your business?

- What services will you provide?

- What size is the market you will serve?

- Who is your competition?

- What price does the competition charge?

- What services does the competition offer?

- How does the competition market their services?

- What will be the price of your service?

- How will you market your services?

- What makes you different or special?

- What will your expenses be to operate your business?

- How will you staff your company for growth?

- What is your growth plan for one year, three years, and five years?

Office Plan

Whether you are working from a spare room at home or renting commercial office space, you need to do some planning for equipment, expenses, insurance, staffing, etc. This should be covered in your business plan. Although a beginning startup business may not seem that significant, it can be costly to set up. (See Chapter 4, The Office.)

REAL ESTATE MARKET RESEARCH

This is the most important part of business planning: who, what, where, when, why, and how much. Who are your customers, and what are their demographics? Are you doing inspections in a high-end area where giving the white-glove treatment is important, or are you in an area of first-time homebuyers where hand-holding and education wins customers? Inspectors often forget to research the types of homes they will be inspecting until they get their first job. Then they are surprised when they encounter, for example, pools/spas, ponds, wells, septic systems, and crawl spaces. Knowing your marketplace is critical to success and survival.

Understanding the Number of Transactions in Your Area

This is just another part of your market research. How many inspections will you need to earn a comfortable living? How many inspections can you do each month? Do you want to build a large multi-inspector firm or stay personal with a single inspector shop? Once you make these decisions, will your marketplace support your needs/desires? How many homes are sold each month in the area in which you plan to work? How many inspectors are already working in that area? As an example: If 60 homes are sold each month in your service area and you want to perform 30 inspections a month at $400 per inspection, that is possible. But what if there are already three inspectors in your marketplace charging $350 per inspection? Will it be difficult to take work away from them at an increased inspection price? Of course it will. Another example: What if only 20 homes in your service area are sold each month and you want 30? You will have to market in surrounding areas and spend more time driving to create your business. This is a basic part of creating an inspection business that many people do not consider. Know how many homes are sold, how many inspectors you must compete with, how much the inspection fees are in the area, and what your business goals are. With all this knowledge, you will be better equipped to make your business a success.

UNDERSTANDING REAL ESTATE DOCUMENTS

What really drives the inspection business? Is it buyers wanting help understanding home conditions, or is it sellers and agents wanting to shed liability with disclosure issues? It wasn't until the advent of the real estate transfer disclosure requirements from state to state that the home inspection business became popular. In 1976, a lawsuit filed by a buyer against the seller and broker over the lack of disclosure of the home's condition brought about the need for home inspections. This lawsuit, *Easton v. Strassburger*, ended in 1984 and was a landmark case. Disclosure laws rolled out state by state requiring seller disclosure and broker inspections of properties that were being sold. Home inspection was one way to deflect some of this liability, and the profession grew. As a home inspector, understanding where you fit into a real estate transaction is important. You should read the real estate purchase documents to see how everything is written and look for opportunities that other inspectors may not have seen.

The Documents

If you already know an agent, ask for a copy of the standard agreements associated with a residential property sale. The better you know the contracts, the more intelligent you will appear to agents and brokers when marketing your business to them. Here are a few of the documents you should familiarize yourself with:

> **Listing Contract:** the agreement between the broker and seller stating the term of the listing and commission percentage.
> **Property Disclosure Statement:** the document the seller completes indicating what he or she knows about the property. In most states, this form is mandatory.
> **Real Estate Agent Disclosure Form:** the document the selling agent is required to provide to the buyer stating that he or she is working for the seller.
> **Offer to Purchase Form and Amendments:** the form submitted by the buyer to the seller stating the agreed-upon sales price. The Amendments usually include the home inspection contingency.

AGENT RESEARCH

Research is critical to getting your business started, learning the marketing niches for inspection calls, and knowing what techniques or information is tired and ineffective in your area. Your goal is to develop a contact database to draw from when marketing. This database is your primary tool for managing and maintaining the relationships you establish. Use the following steps to create your contact database.

Step 1: Find a Real Estate Agent or Broker to Help

You probably already know an agent or a broker who would be willing to help you get your business up and running. Your goal should be to work with an agent who is a key player in the market and will help you identify your targets. The agent's experience and success will help you because he or she knows who is who in the marketplace.

If you do not know someone fitting this description, network with your acquaintances until you find someone who can lead you to this agent or broker. Ask for the following information:

- Which 10% to 20% of the offices are doing 80% to 90% of the business?

- Who are the top performing broker/owners and agents in that group? Try to get as many names as possible, ideally 25 to 50 names.

- Ask permission to use the person's name when contacting these agents. Name-dropping is the essence of business networking, as people tend to trust the referrals of people they already know, like, and trust.

Step 2: Get a List of Agents from the MLS

Most local Boards of REALTORS® have a book that lists all of the agents and agencies registered as members. If you cannot gain access to this book through the local board you belong to or an agent you know, try looking on your state's regulating agency's website. In most states, agents' licensing is a matter of public record and is available in a downloadable text file.

The list should include business addresses and telephone numbers. If the list is from the state licensing agency, it may include information regarding license status.

Step 3: Prioritize the First (Personal) List

Arrange the names as follows:

- Broker/agencies in order of size from the most agents to the fewest.

- Agents by the largest to smallest offices.

This is your personal networking list of the agents you want to meet when making your first visits to the offices. You were instructed to prioritize the agents according to the size of their offices because once contact is made and they agree to call you for an inspection, they are in a position to refer you to other agents in their offices. The bigger the office, the greater the impact on your inspection volume.

Step 4: Prioritize the Second List

As with the personal networking list, go through the MLS list you obtained from the state's website or the MLS book and prioritize the offices in the same order, that is, from largest to smallest. Have your contact help you identify the top producing offices on that list.

Step 5: Prepare Your Affiliate List

Repeat the process above with each of the following affiliates:

- Mortgage brokers
- Bankers
- Title agents

Record Keeping

You now have three lists:

1. **Personal** Contacts

2. **Master** Office List

3. **Affiliate** List

Keep these lists up to date and use database software to track the agents, offices, and affiliates. Use the database to document your conversations, follow-up reminders, referrals, and inspections performed. Accurate documentation of your contacts will come in handy six months from now when you want to review your contacts and mine the data from the software according to results or inspections.

Having this information can further develop your business by identifying what you are doing right and which efforts are most productive. The end result will be more effective marketing in the future, when your business is growing and you have less time for marketing. The more you know about how to be effective, the more targeted your marketing becomes. As a result, you can spend less time being more effective in your marketing efforts, leaving your schedule open for more inspections.

A very important element of marketing to your referral base is to keep excellent records of each real estate company. You can start by making up a single agent file containing an Agent Record Sheet for each real estate company. It's also a good idea to copy the company's listing from the front of the MLS book and staple it to this sheet. That way you'll have the list of all the agents for that company on hand.

A single file of all real estate agents should work in the beginning. But later in your marketing process, you may accumulate enough additional information about each agent to start individual files.

NOTE: Agents tend to move from real estate company to real estate company, so these record sheets will have to be updated periodically.

Not Every Agent Is a REALTOR®

REALTOR® (pronounced Real-tor, not Real-a-tor) is the trademarked name of members of the National Association of REALTORS® (NAR), the largest trade association of real estate agents and brokers in the nation with over 1 million members. Another mistake is to call all real estate agents Realtors. A person must be a member of NAR to hold this designation, so be aware of what you say and how you say it.

If you cannot gain access to the MLS information, you may have to dig deeper. This may consist of scanning the local newspapers and homes-for-sale magazines for homes listed for sale and the agents or brokers who listed them as well as doing an online search. You should search for those agents with the largest advertisement. Also look for ads that show the agents' awards for being the top seller or part of the millionaires club of the agency. You want agents who are top sellers.

You also can search several websites to find top selling agents. Following are a few examples.

www.realtrends.com/rankings/real-trends-1000-individuals-by-volume
www.realtrends.com/rankings/real-trends-1000-teams-by-volume
www.realtrends.com/rankings/real-trends-1000-individuals-by-sides
www.realtrends.com/rankings/real-trends-500-by-sides

You also should search your local area for real estate agents and brokers' websites.

Affiliated Business Persons

Follow these steps to list people in associated businesses who can form a part of your referral base.

1. Find a mortgage banker to help you. Find someone you know personally or have your banker introduce you to someone. Arrange a meeting with him or her.

2. Have the banker give you a list of personal names. Again, for the purpose of developing a list of personal contacts, get the names of bankers,

mortgage brokers, attorneys, appraisers, etc., whom the banker knows handle many of the real estate transactions in the area.

3. Have the banker help you prioritize List 3, the list of personal contacts. The banker should be able to help you rearrange these names in order of most important to contact to least important.

4. Have the banker help you prioritize List 4, the list of affiliates. The MLS book should list all affiliates to the Board of REALTORS®. Ask the banker to help you prioritize this list from most important to contact to least important. Mark those affiliates that also appear in List 3.

5. List all bankers and mortgage brokers for List 5. This is a list of all the bankers and mortgage brokers in your area. You can find them in the phone book or online.

JOINING REAL ESTATE ASSOCIATIONS AND LOCAL REAL ESTATE BOARDS

Brokers and agents can be members of a professional organization called the **National Association of REALTORS®** (NAR). The organization has a **Board of REALTORS®** for each state in each local area. The local Board of Realtors holds meetings on a regular basis, probably monthly, to present topics that are important to their members and hosts social gatherings. Almost all of the big real estate companies belong to it.

Each local Board of REALTORS® offers an **affiliate membership** to people in businesses related to the real estate process, such as home inspection companies, lending institutions, attorneys, appraisers, and title companies. It is highly recommended that your home inspection company becomes an affiliate of all local Boards of REALTORS® in the areas you serve and that you maintain that affiliation with a high profile.

Joining the local Board of REALTORS® means that your home inspection company is kept up to date on real estate issues and that you can socialize with brokers, agents, and other affiliates. This important part of the networking process is required to build a strong referral base.

Make sure you attend the local meetings as a means of staying in touch with people. Try to get on one of the board's committees and become actively involved with the group. The Boards of REALTORS® will have numerous groups where your assistance is valuable, such as a consumer protection group or an affiliate liaison group. Volunteer your time and contribute to the groups however you can.

If the board has breakfasts or weekly meetings, make sure you attend. If you are an affiliate, you may be allowed to introduce yourself to the group. Imagine every week or month being able to stand in front of the real estate agents and tell them who you are and what your company name is. If you are consistent with your appearances, you will quickly be recognized as a regular part of the real estate community.

Also be sure to attend any social outings the group plans, such as holiday dinner dances and golf outings. You may want to become a sponsor of as many events as you can, such as a hole-in-one contest at a golf outing or the barbeque cooking at a local event.

Why Is All This Important?

The importance of becoming part of your local real estate community cannot be overemphasized in relation to achieving success with your home inspection business. Even though it is possible to attract business directly from homebuyers and other consumers, the fastest way to the money is through the real estate community. Agents work hard to control their transaction (as well they should because it is their client) and make it as smooth and professional as possible. The real estate transaction has many moving parts and requires many outside services to complete, including you, the home inspector.

There is also a desire on the agent's part to work with people the agent **trusts** to do the best job for the agent and his or her clients. Imagine having a home inspector working for your client that you do not know or do not like or even worse do not trust. Any of those are problems that most agents work hard to avoid. So getting people to trust you is the key. And how do you do that if people don't know you or have never met you.

This is the circle you must complete:

Know – Like – Trust – Work

How is it possible for me to work with you if I do not know you?
How is it possible for me to like you if I do not know you?
How is it possible for me to trust you if I do not know you or like you?

Because all parts hinge on the agents knowing you, getting out and meeting agents is critical. Consistently being around agents and at their events helps them to recognize you and get to know you. Sitting with and speaking to agents helps them to get to know you and possibly like you enough to work with you. But getting to know people well by working together on committees or in groups at their association's events builds the trust that is needed to secure their business and refer you to their clients.

UNDERSTANDING THE COMPETITION'S OFFERINGS

Market research was discussed earlier, mentioning that you need to know everything about those already doing inspections in your service area. This information will be invaluable to you for many reasons. You should perform a survey of your competition in a few ways. Go under cover and start calling every inspection company, acting as a homebuyer or real estate agent who is looking for information about ordering an inspection. Ask every inspector in your area the following questions:

> **What is your price?** Ask for pricing for the same house each time so that you can compare each company. Make it complex so that you can see if the company charges for extras. For example, ask for a quote for a 2400-square-foot two-story home on a raised foundation; the house is 53 years old and has a pool/spa and a septic system. This variety of conditions can change the price of the inspection.
>
> **What additional services do you offer?** Find out if your competition offers any other services besides home inspections—services such as testing for mold, air quality, and energy efficiency.

What is your experience? Knowing whom you are going to compete against is critical. Some inspectors simply sell their time doing inspections. You need to know who the old-timers as well as the newbies are in your area.

What is your USP? USP is short for unique selling proposition. What makes inspectors different or special, and how do they position themselves during their sales pitch? While you have each inspector on the phone, listen carefully as you talk to them about their inspection service. What are they saying about themselves to make you believe they are better than the other companies? What are they offering you that is unique or special? Do they provide you with an inspection warranty? Do they deliver the inspection report on-site? Compared with other inspectors, do they do anything different? Do they say that they are specialists in old houses? Are they doing environmental testing? Take notes so that when you review them later, you will know how to compete with them in conducting inspections.

Create a spreadsheet of your surveys and make sure you record all your work. This worksheet will help you know what other inspectors are charging, what extra services they provide, and what makes them different or special. This information will help you determine what is important in creating a successful business in your marketplace or might even show you some openings or opportunities that others overlooked.

You might try a couple of surveys—one as a buyer and one as a real estate agent—to see if the inspectors approach the call in different ways. You might be surprised at the results. When calling as an agent, you might ask them to send you a sample report as well as their marketing brochures.

Your next undercover job is to review your competition's websites. This may take some time, but you will learn a great deal of information about inspectors, such as how long they have been in business, what services they provide, whether they accept credit cards, and whether you can order an inspection online. The competition's website will be a gold mine of information, but you must do both types of research. The way a company answers its phone is critical in the inspection business.

The next research project is to survey as many real estate agents as possible and find out which home inspection companies they choose and why. What the agents think about inspectors is critical, and you may discover something you can change or add to your service that increases business.

UNDERSTANDING HOME INSPECTION LAWS IN YOUR AREA (WHAT STANDARDS ARE REQUIRED)

When creating a home inspection business, you must know the minimum standards of practice (SOPs) for your area or state. Many states currently have licensing or regulations on home inspectors. If the standards by which you are to perform an inspection are regulated, you must know those rules and follow them diligently. Working in a state with regulations and not knowing them is no excuse in a courtroom. These are laws by which you must live and work. Those rules will also help you understand what you must do for your clients and what is not required. If your state does not have regulations, then whatever your competition is doing or whatever the predominant association standards are in your area will be the standards you should go by.

Joining a state or national association will be valuable for you in several ways. First, as a practicing home inspector, you want to be around other home inspectors, and an association is the best place to find others who do what you want to do. Also, associations set forth SOPs for their members that you can learn from and adopt as your own (providing your state does not have any).

SOPs are important because they define your job. SOPs tell you what you must do and what you are not required to do. Make sure you follow the requirements but don't overlook the things you are not required to do because there may be some hidden opportunities for your business. If others are not including something in their inspections that clients are requesting, you might have a unique selling opportunity if you can provide it.

How to Determine What Inspections or Services Are Best for You to Offer? Can You Find Opportunity in the Things That You Aren't Required to Do?

As mentioned, you have a set minimum standard of care that you must follow to provide your clients with a standard home inspection. That does not mean you must do only those required things. You can opt to provide more; you just need to be qualified, trained, and sometimes licensed to provide those additional services during your home inspection.

For instance, one thing you cannot do is engineering on the home unless you are a licensed engineer. But even then, you are not doing engineering during an inspection unless it was specifically requested by your client and you are qualified to provide that service on whatever you are asked to check. Engineering requires calculations and analysis far beyond the scope of a home inspection.

Mold testing, however, is a service that many inspectors provide after they receive proper training. Also, if their state requires a license, they must obtain that credential. But many states don't regulate mold testing or radon testing or other environmental services, so these are additional options for inspectors. Just make sure you are trained and qualified to provide the extra services with your home inspections.

Looking for Trends and Changes. What's Next?

Success is found in trends and changes. As stated earlier, home inspection grew because of a change in the regulations and procedures of the real estate transaction. Someone got sued, and the decisions of that lawsuit were so important that the real estate community embraced the home inspection profession and included it as an option in the purchase of a home. The home inspection business went from being used by a small number of homebuyers to being used in nearly 80% of all homes sold. Home inspectors sometimes overlook this change or don't realize it occurred, but this caused a billion dollar industry to be born. So why aren't home inspectors looking for more trends and changes?

You work in the real estate industry. That industry is always changing the rules and creating opportunity. For instance, a few years ago in California, the requirement was added that whenever a house was sold, the water heater had to be strapped for earthquakes. Did that rule change create an opportunity to strap water heaters?

Be mindful of what your real estate laws require, what the paperwork has on the issues, and how you might be able to satisfy those needs. Assume that the purchase document states that it is up to the buyer to research any building permits for the home he or she is purchasing. What if a buyer does not know how to do this? Is this an opportunity to offer an additional service with your inspection? Many services will be brought to light in the real estate purchase documents. Stay informed and you might see some opportunities come your way.

FEASIBILITY

Extra services can require extra training and extra work. You must analyze everything thoroughly before jumping in. You need to answer the following questions before you begin adding extra services or even doing inspections:

- What will you need to provide the services you want to offer?

- What are the training or license requirements?

- Will you make money? Is it worth the extra work?

- Are competitors doing it? If so, will you need this service just to compete with them?

- Will this help you with differentiation?

- Will this help sell your service better than your competition does?

- What makes you unique? This is the beginning of coming up with your USP to outsell your competition.

- Can you price your services to make money? Will they just be loss leaders to gain you more work?

- Will these extra services take more of your time? Will they be cost-effective for you to deliver?

- Can you still provide a quality home inspection while trying to offer additional services? Will your level of service be affected?

- All of this ties in to your market research. Understanding your competition, what they offer, and what they sell is critical to surviving.

Some other considerations for your inspection service:

Time to do the inspection   This does not mean you have enough time to do an inspection; it means how long will it take you to perform each inspection. A seasoned inspector knows how to get around a house in a standard amount of time. The typical time for a 2000-square-foot single-story home that is 10 years or newer and on a slab foundation is around 2.5 hours. If you are taking longer, people may be upset, or if you are not spending enough time, you may be missing things. The amount of time spent on an inspection is important.

Number of inspectors per inspection   The norm is one inspector per home inspection, right? Today, teams of inspectors are growing across the country. A franchise is even named HomeTeam. This does not mean that you must have a team; it is just another trend to watch and be aware of.

Inspection warranty   Another trend in the inspection profession is to offer a limited warranty with your home inspection. This can be a short-term warranty or guaranty that the items you inspected are and will remain the way you said they were for a period of time. Most inspection warranties are around 90 to 100 days from the date of the inspection and have low limits of coverage, such as $500. Inspectors can create and offer their own warranty for their inspections at little to no cost. Your warranty can help you differentiate your service from others or help you compete with those already providing this. There is a service called Warranty Management LLC, a service designed by inspectors to help inspectors manage their own warranty programs.

Extras given at inspection [book, video, membership to Home Owners Network (HON)]   Many inspectors provide great value with every inspection. Just the act of doing the inspection can be of tremendous value for the buyer when he or she negotiates repairs on the things the inspector found to be deficient. However, some inspectors find that giving added value to their clients results in faster referrals. Giving clients a home maintenance book, manual, or video can be this added value that makes your clients remember you. Giving memberships to HON also can be a huge value for your clients, gaining you more referrals because of the branding HON provides inspectors. Check out the services at www.homeownersnetwork.com or look at www.simplebooklet.com /honinspectors for details.

MARKETING HOME INSPECTIONS

Marketing home inspections is similar to planting a tomato garden in your backyard. Typically, tomatoes take about 90 days to go from seeds to fruit on the vine. If you want to have a steady, consistent crop of tomatoes during the growing season, you need to organize your garden into segments and plant every few weeks while tending to the vines already planted.

Here is an explanation: It takes about 90 days from the time a real estate agent meets a client and reaches a listing agreement or buyer representation agreement to the time everyone arrives at the closing table for the keys to change hands.

How does this affect your marketing? The people you meet today may not need a home inspector for another 90 day. There will be agents/brokers along the way that you meet earlier in the 90-day cycle who call for your services, but 90 days is typically when you can expect your marketing efforts to begin to pay dividends. Ninety days is when first-time *and* repeat business can roll in simultaneously.

As with a tomato garden, home inspectors have to be scattering seeds continuously throughout the real estate community. No one ever arrives in this business and gets to stop marketing. A home inspector who is not constantly visible to agents and brokers is a home inspector who watches his or her business decline rapidly in less than the 90 days it took to get it there. With that in mind, you can begin to build your marketing campaign.

Top Referral Sources for Home Inspectors

The answer to the question of who refers us the most is real estate agents and brokers. *They refer their clients to inspectors they know and trust.* A good encounter with an agent/broker should lead to a long-term relationship. Do the right things and you will create long-lasting relationships with many agents and brokers on which to build your business.

We will be talking in terms of a "campaign." The word *campaign* means "Work in an organized and active way toward a particular goal." You should think in terms of a campaign to build and maintain your business goals. Organize your marketing to become more effective and to be better received by the real estate community.

Once you begin the marketing campaign, start building your business with some top producing agents. How do you find them?

- Refer to office publications (Agent-of-the-Month or Agent-of-the-Year announcements)

- Ask other top producers.

- Look in the Real Estate section of the newspaper.

Other referral sources to work on a few weeks into your marketing campaign include bankers and mortgage brokers, title agencies, insurance agents, and attorneys. Although the bulk of your business will come from real estate agents, professionals in related industries are in a position to refer clients your way and shouldn't be taken for granted.

Business Networking

Another way to find quality referrals is through business networking groups. These are groups of business professionals who meet weekly to exchange referrals and to stay in touch.

An unfortunate aspect of these organizations is that they limit access to the group to one representative from each profession. In other words, you would be the only home inspector in the group, and likewise, there would be only one real estate agent, if there was one at all. These networking groups are beneficial in some ways but limiting in others.

As a new home inspector trying to ramp up business as quickly as possible, you may find membership in these groups to be less than cost-effective and decide to focus on other more affordable ways to build your business in the first year. A worldwide association for business networking is BNI. Its website is www.bni.com. There you will find links to local chapters in your area.

Marketing Points

There are some key things you need to know and understand while beginning and maintaining your marketing campaign—the marketing points. These are points you refer to when trying to determine whether to participate in a marketing function or to experiment with a technique that wasn't covered in this manual.

In the early stages of establishing your business, you may get discouraged from hearing agents tell you that they already have a favorite inspector or that business is down this year. Not to worry; all inspectors hear these things regardless of the condition of the economy or whether they've been in business five months or five years.

When you are considering additional strategies (or you want to avoid getting discouraged), there are a few things to remember:

Point 1: Your competitors offer the same services as you.

There will always be competition. Don't get discouraged because you see a stack of other brochures in offices or when agents tell you they already have an inspector.

The difference separating you from most of the competition is that you are AHIT-certified and have been trained to exceed the industry or state SOPs on every inspection you perform. In addition, you have access to industry experience and knowledge through an ongoing technical support program that allows you to pick up the phone and call with a technical question anytime during business hours.

Point 2: In the beginning, the buyer's inspection will be 100% of your business.

This will be the core of your business. Do your best to avoid becoming distracted. Remember, you're a farmer planting seeds and tending the crops, not a hunter/gatherer.

What's the difference? Farmers have a plan and a strategy for maximizing their crops by timing the planting and harvests. Farmers knows that they'll have to store up finances and supplies for the winter when there is no crop to feed their family.

Hunters/gatherers *plan* to hide in the bushes with spear in hand waiting for the woolly mammoth to come along so that they can feed and clothe their families for the winter. If they have to wait long enough, a rabbit may scurry by and their hunger distracts them. As a result, they hunt down the rabbit so that they can eat *now*, causing them to potentially miss the opportunity of the larger animal.

Each approach has its merits in the appropriate business setting, and AHIT's experience has been that the farmer approach works best when establishing relationships on which to build a home inspection business.

Point 3: Clients will come to you almost exclusively from your referral base.

For many businesses, radio and TV advertising are an effective way to reach the masses and bring business through the door. For home inspectors, these traditional advertising outlets are not as cost-effective. In other words, what you pay for the production and airtime far exceeds the return you will see in inspection revenues.

Point 4: What are sales and marketing?

- Marketing

  The term used most often in this manual is *marketing*. This is what entrepreneurs in many service-oriented businesses must do to bring customers to their business. It's the act of encouraging customers to inquire about and ultimately choose your services over the competition. Everything you do ultimately boils down to marketing your services. Preparing the brochures and business cards as well as performing the inspection and documenting a report in clear, easy-to-understand language has the potential to entice others to call you for their next home inspection.

Most of what you focus on is marketing because it represents the majority of your activities when you are building your business. And in your business, before you can sell your services, you have to market *yourself.*

- Sales

  Sales is the act of persuading a client to make a purchase. You will do some sales as a home inspector. It comes when you are on the phone talking to a customer, sharing the features of your company and asking the customer to schedule an appointment. Remember that you are selling yourself all the time.

Point 5: What are features and benefits?

When marketing, it is helpful to understand the difference between features and benefits. The features of using your services result in benefits to the client. For example, when you do an office presentation for a group of real estate agents, you should discuss a list of features about your new business followed by the *benefits* that agents and brokers will realize from them. (See the script for an office presentation provided in Chapter 3.)

In the presentation, you first capture the audience's attention by explaining that you're going to share the top six reasons agents use your firm. Next, you share the first reason, the on-site report, followed by the benefits to agents, including the easy-to read-format, clear language, and fast delivery of the report.

In your marketing efforts throughout your career, remember to present yourself and your services with regard to features first, followed by the benefits. When delivered in a clear, relaxed tone to your audience, this technique leads to phone calls and ultimately more inspections.

Point 6: What are customers buying?

Many students ask the question, "Why do I have to talk so much about all of these things to agents? Shouldn't they want to call me just because I'm a good home inspector and don't miss the defects that could cost the client a lot of money?"

To answer that question, it's helpful to understand the answer to this other question: "What is the homebuyer really purchasing?" That question can be answered with a few words for each of the most common types of home inspections performed.

Buyer Inspections

- Emotions

  The client probably has seen the home a couple of times before you do. The client chose the home for a reason, and regardless of why he or she chose it, it is his or her new castle.
  Your home inspection report reinforces the reasons the client bought the home, provides a new perspective on the purchase decision, and can be used as a negotiating tool.

- Peace of mind

  Purchasing a home knowing that it has no major defects gives the buyer peace of mind. In situations where conditions requiring repair are found, the report provides a means to get them repaired or consideration for repairs written into the contract.

- A safe environment in which to raise children

  Everyone wants a safe environment in which to raise his or her children. Even families or homeowners without children need to know that they are safe in their new home.

- Solutions

  Although you should avoid documenting and recommending specific repairs or estimating costs to repair the conditions, you still can provide solutions for the buyer through the home inspection report.

  The solutions are in the form of recommending the appropriate technician with whom to consult for the repairs. With so many emotions and issues to think about when purchasing a home (home selection, financing, moving logistics, negotiations, etc.), the realization that some major repairs are in order can easily overwhelm a buyer.

As a result, thinking about whom to call for repairs can be confusing, especially when most homeowners do not understand how a repair should be made. The inspection report provides permanent documentation of what needs to be repaired and what type of professional is most qualified to do it.

The important thing to remember is that the client is buying the *benefits* of a home inspection, not the *features*. Your technical skills are a feature to agents and their clients. It's assumed that your technical skills are up to the level expected. There is no way for agents and clients to verify your skills other than to observe you during the inspection process and listen to your verbal summary.

With more states enacting licensing laws for home inspectors (and associations such as ASHI, NAHI, and NACHI), the importance of a home inspector's technical qualifications takes a backseat to how well he or she communicates the findings to the client.

Agents know that they *can* judge you by your ability to communicate, your demeanor, and your level of professionalism, as well as how you describe the defects and conditions, thus forming a general opinion as to how well you represent your clients. As a result, your marketing efforts should focus on the features first and benefits second when marketing to your number one referral source. This isn't to say you can be a great presenter, marketing specialist, and salesperson only to follow up with a poor home inspection and still expect longevity in the industry. Remember, you get only one first impression, so practice every aspect of your home inspection presentation before doing your first one in front of agents and clients.

Seller (Listing) Inspection

A listing inspection is ordered by a homeowner listing a house for sale. Typically, an agreement has been signed with a real estate agent to represent the homeowner in advertising, marketing, and attracting potential buyers to the property. The seller is locked into an exclusive arrangement, and in the case of a listing inspection, the agent has recommended that the seller get a home inspection to enhance the transaction and speed up the closing process.

For the listing inspection, your client is looking for the benefits mentioned previously, with a few added features:

- Saving money

    Most home sellers can expect a buyer to order a home inspection once an agreement has been reached. A proactive means to saving money is through a listing inspection.

    Without a looming 10-day deadline, the seller can take more time to focus on items needing repair, negotiate bids with technicians for repairs, and decide which items may not be worth repairing. Knowing in advance the items not worth repairing prepares the seller for the negotiations and avoids sacrificing valuable equity in the home for the sake of meeting the negotiation deadline and the possibility of losing a buyer.

- Eliminating surprises

    As discussed in the technical course, many homeowners are unaware of all the conditions the inspector can find in a home. Surprises in the home inspection report tend to drive emotions up and have the potential to kill a deal.

    A proactive home inspection eliminates these surprises and builds a more confident transaction.

- Full compliance with disclosure laws

    Every state has disclosure laws regarding the seller's knowledge of past or current conditions on the property. A professional home inspection report satisfies the seller's requirement to disclose anything he or she knows about the property.

    So what's the benefit to this feature?

- Minimizes the possibility of a nondisclosure lawsuit against the seller after a sale.

    Even with the liability shield a home inspector provides, a homeowner and his or her agent can be subject to a lawsuit when undisclosed major defects are discovered after the sale. The report minimizes the possibility of a post-sale lawsuit by providing documentation and written proof that everything was done to uncover major defects.

- Minimizes negative emotions

    As you know, emotions tend to run high during the sale of a home. The agents have invested their time, money, and efforts into the client; the buyers have run the gamut of emotions throughout the selection, qualification, and appraisal processes; and the sellers have seen their share of traffic through the home and may have had a deal on the table that was lost for various reasons, such as financing, repairs, or buyer's remorse. Once a home inspector's report is on the table, sellers can be surprised about some or all of the findings. Whether through a lack of knowledge or any other reason, the surprise can raise a number of concerns. Will the buyer try to renegotiate? How much will it cost to fix some of the items in the report? Will the buyer walk away from the deal based on what was found? These are just a few of the concerns, and each can result in stress and anxiety for the seller. A professional home inspection at the listing of the property is proactive and exposes concerns in advance, allowing the seller to prepare a position to take about repairs in advance of a negotiated contract.

- Results in a faster closing

  Many times, with the home inspection done in advance, an agreement can be reached as to the repairs and sale price of the home without a buyer's inspection.

  The 10-day inspection contingency is often amended to any number of additional days when the inspection is scheduled toward the end of the original 10 days.

  Should the buyer choose to rely on the report and waive his or her rights to a buyer's inspection, the traditional 10-day inspection contingency is eliminated and the end result is fewer days to closing.

  All of these *features* create the *benefit* of peace of mind for the seller and the buyer resulting from the listing inspection.
  Other types of inspections were discussed in Chapter 1.

MARKETING PLAN

This section provides information, training programs and scripts, and follow-up activities designed to sell home inspection services to customers.

An important principle is that "nothing will come from nothing." You already know what this means, but relate it to building a home inspection business. If you expect orders to come in even though you have done little to no marketing, then you are starting the wrong business—or any business for that matter. The principle of actions create actions is one you must embrace. The home inspection business drives itself on activity by inspectors. Those activities are designed to get real estate agents and brokers to know you. Once you are known, you have to build trust. Think about it for a minute: An agent makes a living from selling homes. Agents must close sales to survive. As an agent would you give your client to a home inspector you had never met or knew nothing about? How can you expect work to come your way if no one knows who you are? The steps are simple: Meet agents and get to know them. Build as much trust with as many agents as you can. Build trust by becoming friends with them. Friendship builds trust. If an agent does not know you, he or she will not use you. It is that simple for agents.

So if it is that simple, why don't more inspectors get out there and meet agents? Finding places to meet agents is the hard part. Or is it?

Here's a list of where to find real estate agents:

- Real estate offices

- Open houses

- Board of REALTOR® meetings

- Charity events

- Networking groups

- Facebook

- LinkedIn

MAIN PRINCIPLES OF HOME INSPECTION MARKETING

These are the main operating principles behind the marketing plan presented in this section. These are the points you need to keep in mind once you make with a prospective customer.

- Remember: Customers shop for a home inspector just like they shop for many products—looking for the best price. Most agents will give their clients brochures and business cards of three or four home inspection companies. When potential customers call your office, because this may be the first time they have ordered a home inspection, they really have no idea what they are looking for or what questions to ask. They may think they're shopping for price, but you need to show them how professional your company is and that you can do a good job for them. You should give them the right questions to ask you or any other inspectors they might call.

- Remember: Getting the appointment is not automatic. Callers are shoppers. They're not going to call and simply ask for an appointment. What happens on the phone when a prospective customer calls your office is called sales. Your objective is to capture the appointment. You do this through the professional treatment of the caller, by educating them about home inspection, and by building confidence in your company's ability to do a good job for them.

- Remember: You're in a communications business. All of the business of a home inspection company is conducted in a communications mode.

  NOTE: Become an educator. Customers usually need to be educated. In some areas of the country, the public's awareness is quite low of what a home inspection is. Unless customers have bought or sold a home in the last 20 years, they may not know what a home inspection is. They may not understand what happens during the home inspection, what role it plays in the inspection, and what a home inspector is like. They may not understand that home inspectors are highly trained professionals with both technical and communications skills. Therefore, education is a large part of the customer marketing plan. This is true before, during, and after an inspection. The role of your company as an educator doesn't stop.

- Use your people skills. Being able to communicate, being personable and patient, and being helpful and sensitive to what customers are going through—all of these skills will serve schedulers and inspectors well.

Remember that people in the midst of a real estate transaction have a lot at stake. They can be nervous, suspicious, and frightened.

- Form relationships with customers. The scheduler and the inspector are professionals, but that doesn't mean they are cold and impersonal. A scheduler is a helper who sorts out the details, teaches callers about home inspection, and makes appointments to fit the customer's busy schedule. The inspector is a trusted technician who educates the customer about the process and findings, takes responsibility for the customer's understanding, wants to do a good job for the customer, and clearly works for the customer. These are relationships.

- Provide excellent services. This principle doesn't come last because it's least important. Nothing helps sales more than doing an excellent job for customers. It opens the door for selling other products and services to satisfied customers. It also brings you more customers by word of mouth. Satisfied customers have a way of letting other people know about you.

ELEMENTS OF THE MARKETING PLAN

The first step in developing a customer marketing plan is to be clear about what you want the plan to accomplish. What are your goals? There are basically three goals in customer marketing:

1. To capture customer appointments for the basic services you offer

2. To upsell customers on additional services you offer

3. To sell products and services to previous customers and the general public, such as the Home Maintenance Inspection Program and mold testing

The customer marketing plan describes in detail what should be done to accomplish your goals. Your marketing plan should be your guide as to what you will be doing each day, week, or month to generate phone calls and when you will be doing it. Unlike the inspectors questioned who did not have clear answers to what they did that week to make the phone ring, you will be following an action plan to create business.

Here are some basic steps to follow:

- Set some realistic goals for your business.

    —How many inspections would you like in the next 12 months?

    - If you want 240 inspections in a year, that means 20 inspections per month, or one a day five days a week.

    —How many real estate agents must you know to generate that many inspections?

    - If the average real estate agent sells 12 homes a year, you need 60 solid agents referring you to their clients. Agents typically give their clients a list of three inspectors from which to choose, so figuring you can close up to three phone calls, you have 20 inspections a month.

- If you concentrate on finding the top producing agents in your area and get them to refer you, your business can grow faster with fewer agents. A top producer could be selling 30 to 50 homes a year.

—How long will it take to get 60 real estate agents to know, like, trust, and refer you?

- Each day you need to meet multiple real estate agents. You need to impress them enough that they are interested in using your services.

- Create a daily plan for getting in front of agents. This will include office visits, presentations, and Board of Realtor meetings

—How long will it take to create a consumer following?

- Your website is critical, but so is your image and recognition as an expert.

- Press releases are important in building your image.
  - Press release can be about you, your training, and how you are starting your business
  - Press releases can be about home care topics. You want to be the home inspection expert, so creating that image is important.
  - Published press releases can show your credibility to the real estate community.

—How much social networking can you do?
- Create a business Facebook account.
- Create a LinkedIn account.
- Begin social networking.

• Create a realistic timeline and calendar for your marketing.

—How many offices will you visit each week/day?

—How many agents can you meet each week/day?

- Where will you meet them?
  - Open houses
  - Office meetings
  - Local charity events
  - Board meetings
  - Networking groups

—How many press releases can you create each week/month?

- What newspapers, magazines, and online sources will publish you?

—How much social networking can you do each day/week/month?

Make sure that everything you plan has a deadline or due date. Create a schedule for all the goals above; otherwise, you will never do the tasks required to get you the business you deserve. If you know you need 60 agents to make your business a success, you must create a plan to meet and attract those agents.

Here is an example of how your weekly calendar should look:

Monday

- Visit 10 real estate offices and drop off brochures. You also might consider doing something special such as delivering candy or cookies to each office. Many inspectors are trying to get their brochures in the real estate offices, so make sure the agents want to see you each time you visit.

- Contact 20 agents on Facebook and LinkedIn. Then take time to personally send them a letter and/or email. At this point, you are still cold-calling and building your list.

- Contact five family members or friends about your inspection business.

Tuesday

- Many real estate offices hold weekly meetings (Tuesday is popular), so try to get an invitation to those meetings. If you can create a presentation that is beneficial to the agents, you may be allowed to speak, but don't expect to be allowed to make a sales pitch as they don't have the time or desire.

- Write an article for publication in the local newspapers.

- Contact 20 agents on Facebook and LinkedIn. Then take time to personally send them a letter and/or email. At this point, you are still cold-calling and building your list.

- Contact five family members or friends about your inspection business.

Continue planning every day of the week to generate business. If you are sitting in your office wondering why the phone is not ringing, you are not working to get work. Your most important task is to make yourself known and get the phone to ring.

Referrals are the key to success: Knowing one agent helps, but making sure that agent refers you to his or her clients as well as the other agents in the office is critical. You want the first agent to use you and then tell his or her colleagues about you. Will this happen naturally? Probably not. So you need a plan to make sure the other agents in the office see and hear about you. Press for referrals from everyone! Here are some tips to generating more referrals:

- Ask for referrals.

    —Asking people for referrals is the easiest way to generate work, but it is not foolproof.

—Create systems that make getting referrals easier. This means using electronic systems, business cards, and newsletters and constantly staying in touch.

—Send announcements to other agents about working with one of their colleagues (with permission).

—Use an influencing system such as this: Return to the agent's office the day after each inspection with a thank-you gift such as candy; wine; or, better yet, a bouquet of helium balloons with your company name on them. Tie a basket of candy to the bottom of the balloons to hold them over the agent's desk all day. Every agent in the office will see them and your company information.

• Ask everyone you know to give you referrals.

—Tell your family, friends, and acquaintances about your new business.

—Statistically everyone will have six conversations with other people each year about moving. That means for every 10 people who know about your business, you could get 60 referrals. Every 100 people equals 600 referral opportunities.

—Your family and friends will have many opportunities to give you referrals if they know you want them.

—Give everyone you know your business cards and flyers.

WORKING THE MARKETING PLAN

Your company is almost established, and administrative controls and procedures are in place. You have invested time in researching your market to determine pricing and top producing agents, and you know where to find those agents. You also should establish your membership with the local Boards of REALTORS® and get ready for the phones to ring.

What do you do with this wealth of information? All the knowledge and experience in the world can't make the phones ring, so you need to learn how to apply what you've learned.

Preparation

Review the following materials to make sure you have everything:

• Brochures and stands

• Business cards

• Marketing lists

• Giveaway items (pens, scratch pads, candy, etc.)

Make sure you keep plenty of brochures, business cards, and giveaway items (if any) in your inspection vehicle. Protect your marketing materials from damage by rain, snow, dust, and dirt, as well as from damage caused by banging around the vehicle/trunk/truck bed. After all the time and money you invested in your new career, it would be a shame to lose opportunities because the materials look old or are damaged.

Organize the materials for quick and easy access. If you have your signage on the vehicle (as you should—*always*), you will find that people occasionally approach you in parking lots, at gas stations, at schools, and at any other place you happen to be to ask, "Are you a home inspector?" or "Do you inspect new homes?" *Give them a brochure, a card, and a pen!* You can buy card or brochure holders that stick to your window so that people can take a card or brochure without you being there. They are inexpensive and worth having.

Finally, get your marketing lists out. It's time to use them! As an overview, you're going to follow the marketing plan step-by-step as follows:

- Active Marketing

    —Personal visits

    —Office visits

    —Affiliate visits

    —Board of Realtors functions

    —Open house visits

- Passive Marketing

    —Thank-you letters

    —Congratulations letters

    —Follow-up letters

    —Facebook posts

    —LinkedIn connections

Now you will take a look at each of these items in greater detail before you learn to apply them to your marketing plan.

Active versus Passive
Active marketing is where you go out and meet people face to face, chat with them, and share the features and benefits of working with your company. It is related to public relations, where you aren't in a typical marketing situation, but are still working side by side with agents/brokers and affiliates at lunches, office meetings, charitable functions, golf tournaments, etc.

Whenever you are in an active marketing situation, you should dress accordingly. Look around the offices and make a note of the typical office attire. Are the agents in business formal, business casual, or casual attire? Your attire should match or exceed the agents' attire in the office. In other words, you want to meet or exceed the expectations of the agents you present to, but don't want to be condescending.

For example, if the attire at the office where you will be giving a presentation is business casual, you should wear business casual or formal. A good compromise is polished shoes, pressed slacks, a button-down oxford shirt (preferably with your logo embroidered on the chest), and a sport coat.

Passive marketing includes activities such as writing follow-up letters, writing thank-you letters, doing targeted email marketing, posting on Facebook, and creating LinkedIn connections. It also includes your signage, flyers, and giveaway items, even though most of those items require active marketing to get them circulating among your targeted customers.

Targeted Segments

The goal of the marketing plan is to target the top producing real estate agents and the masses simultaneously. In other words, you're going fishing with a pole *and* a net. Why do you do this? Because top producers aren't the *only* producers. To get a higher volume of business sooner rather than later, you need to a good mix of top producers along with steady producers, part-timers, or short-term agents.

The top producers may have many clients with whom they are working, including buyers and sellers. They may not have a buyer ready for a home inspection for a few weeks, and you want to start doing inspections *right away*. It's good to cut your teeth on short-term or part-time agents so that if you do make a rookie mistake, it won't damage a valued relationship.

While reviewing your marketing lists, determine in what order you will visit those offices according to the following:

1. Where you have personal contacts

2. The size of the offices

3. Geographical location

Some home inspectors begin their marketing campaign with offices close to home, branching out to new areas as they expand. This affords them flexibility in working close to home, but it may limit their prospects in the beginning. Make sure you consider this while creating your marketing routes because sometimes just visiting offices close to home will not get you into top producing offices that may be just a little further away.

Personal Contacts

When stopping by real estate offices, ask for the agents whose names you know. If a real estate agent helped you create your target list, ask for him or her specifically; if not, you still should know the names of the agents in the offices you are visiting. (You can go online to find the offices and agents working there.) Ask the receptionist, "Is Eric Kemper in today? A mutual friend suggested I stop by and leave a few items for him." The receptionist will tell you whether the agent is in the office and, if the agent is, will direct you to his or her area.

In some cases, the receptionist will not allow anyone past the desk. Don't take offense at this; it's the receptionist's job and what he or she has been instructed to do. Perhaps too many affiliates have been milling around the office lately or have been a distraction and the office has had to adjust its policies accordingly.

When you encounter this, leave your materials in an envelope and tell the receptionist that you will follow up by telephone with the agent later in the day to make sure he or she got the package. This is a polite way of telling the receptionist that you expect him or her to deliver the materials and that you intend to hold him or her accountable.

When the agent is in, greet him or her with a smile, shake their hand, and introduce yourself. Tell the agent that it's a pleasure to meet them and that another agent asked you to stop by with your materials. Share a few features and benefits and ask for the opportunity to earn a referral. More than likely, the agent will inform you that he or she already has a relationship with a home inspector. Explain that you understand the importance of referring a home inspector the agent can trust and let him or her know that your company is available in case a backup or substitute is needed. After that, it's up to you and your firm to prove you're everything you say you are.

Finally, thank the agent for his or her time, leave a business card, and go back to your vehicle to document your conversation on the Real Estate Office Farming sheet. Once you get home, you can add the items, contacts, and conversations to your database for follow-up.

Office Visits

After you have met the personal contacts from your list (or when entering offices where you have no personal contact), determine where the affiliate materials are placed and leave a brochure stand with 10 to 15 brochures and 15 to 20 business cards. You will likely find that after six months, your business cards are gone but all 15 brochures are still in place. This is to be expected. If your brochures are gone, check to see how many calls you're getting from that office. If the call volume is low or nonexistent, a competitor may have thrown out your materials. Although it's not "normal," it can happen; simply refill the stand with your brochures.

NOTE: As opposed to a brochure stand, you might try a bowl of candy with your brochures neatly tucked around the edge. At the very least, this will get the attention of the agents when they return for a piece of candy.

Keep in mind that one visit to a real estate office in no way assures you of getting business. But repeat visits week after week and month after month will build credibility in the minds of the agents. They see new inspectors come and go all the time. When they first see you or your marketing materials, they may think, "Oh, just another inspector." But after months of seeing you come to their office, they will recognize you as someone who has been around awhile. The point is, keep it up. Creating a long-term business takes time.

Office Presentations

Booking a presentation won't come automatically. It takes work, but isn't hard to do. Many offices have sales meetings on a regular basis, and every office is different. You may find that some offices don't have meetings or only allow affiliates who advertise with them to present to their agents.

You can discover who the contact person is for scheduling speakers for meetings by asking the receptionist, office manager, or broker. If that person is busy, get a phone number and call him or her later in the day. When asking to be scheduled, whether you do it on the phone or in person, remember to smile. Smiling has a direct effect on your tone of voice, even on the phone. Introduce yourself and tell the person with whom you're speaking that you'd like to sponsor breakfast or lunch at the next available office meeting.

Explain that you have a prepared presentation that takes six or seven minutes, followed by a brief question-and-answer session. If you are only going to talk about you and your company, spend the money on the breakfast or lunch. If you have a presentation that is educational and valuable to the agents, you may get the chance to speak without buying anything! The office manager will let you know how the meetings are planned and whether he or she can schedule you in. Make sure you ask how many agents will be present so that you have enough food for everyone.

If the office doesn't have meetings, don't worry. Plenty of other offices do. This is only one aspect of your marketing campaign, and you will reach agents through other means discussed throughout this manual.

In some cases, the office manager may ask you to focus more on something educational than a "pitch" for your company. Review some of the resources you obtained from the AHIT course materials and prepare a brief educational talk about a topic of your choice. The office manager could be asking for an educational topic for many reasons. Affiliates present to agents at sales meetings frequently, and in many cases, they come without a prepared presentation and take more time than was planned.

Giving an educational talk is an opportunity to set you further apart from the competition. You will be giving the agents in the office information and knowledge they can use rather than another boring talk about how great business is going. Prepare handouts and use graphics from the Illustrated Home Image Library you purchased in class to dress up the handouts.

One week prior to your scheduled meeting, stop by the office with a flyer announcing that you will be there to provide breakfast or lunch for the meeting and put one in each agent's box. Come up with a catchy title or phrase for your presentation, such as "Hot Water: Should I Go Tankless?" Within a couple of days of the meeting, order the food based on whether you will be attending a breakfast or lunch meeting. Here are some ideas:

- Bagels and fresh fruit platters

- Muffins

- Deli trays

- Pizza

- Submarine sandwiches

Many affiliates bring doughnuts and pastries, and although people usually like them, agents often show a sincere appreciation for something a little healthier or something different from doughnuts. Display the food as though it were Easter brunch at a five-star resort. Bring plates, napkins, utensils, and condiments and place them in a logical flow: plates and napkins, utensils, food, and *your marketing materials*.

Your goals are to make a lasting impression and to meet, or exceed, agents' expectations. Your marketing opportunities are a reflection of your professionalism on an inspection. Take this opportunity to shine! Keep your presentation to the time allowed and stay until the end of the meeting to answer additional questions and to meet more agents.

When you are new to giving presentations, you must practice a lot. Try giving your first couple of presentations to smaller offices in case you have trouble. Create a presentation that is memorable, valuable, and a little humorous. People like to laugh, and if you are the person making them laugh, they will remember you.

Open Houses

Open houses are a great way to get one-on-one time with real estate agents. Agents hold open houses for two reasons:

1. To attract potential buyers to the property

2. To make contact with potential buyers who are not already working with an agent

For the home inspector, it's an opportunity to make a lasting impression with a Realtor somewhere other than the office or business setting.

During the week, pick up some small gift bags and colored tissue paper. Then buy prepackaged snacks such as trail mix, granola bars, and fruit snacks. If you have some decals with your company logo and phone number, put one on each bag. (You can easily make these at home on a printer using mailing labels.) Stuff some of the tissue paper into the bags and then fill them with the snacks and a bottle of water. Some home inspectors also like to add items such as notepads, crossword puzzle/word search books, magazines, and even lottery scratch tickets. Arrange the items to look neat and attractive and keep them in a secure place so that they are not damaged while you drive from one open house to the next. Now you have a collection of "Agent Survival Kits" to give to agents while they wait for traffic to come to their open house.

Where do you find open houses? One way is to drive around neighborhoods on Saturday and Sunday mornings looking for the Realtor signs advertising "Open House." Some inspectors prefer to look them up in the local newspaper on Saturday morning so that they can plan their day and get to more agents. Some papers also advertise open houses on their online classified websites. Check with your local newspapers or ask your agent contacts where the best place is to find open houses. Real Estate offices will also advertise on their websites open houses their company and agents will be hosting that weekend.

When you get there, remember your manners and use professional courtesy. For example:

1. Never interrupt an agent who is speaking to a customer.

2. Don't barge in. Ring the bell or knock on the door to announce your arrival even if the sign says to come in.

3. Smile and immediately introduce yourself with a business card and a handshake to put the agent at ease.

4. If you have children, consider taking one of them with you. This may sound unusual, as no one wants a rowdy toddler running around a house, but having a child with you may make the agent more comfortable about having you there.

Agents receive training that prepares them for predators and criminals targeting them at open houses or vacant home showings. You do not want to appear as though you're there for any reason other than to network and establish a working relationship. Be professional, don't overstay your welcome, and smile. If your child is with you, have him or her carry the bag and hand it to the agent. Teach your child to smile and say something cute. The agents will love it and remember you for a long time.

Affiliate Visits
Your affiliate visits have less impact and are not as personal as your visits to real estate offices. In other words, most home inspectors do not ask for the opportunity to speak at affiliate offices, but do leave their materials with a key contact.

Although affiliates are not in a position to refer to your company every buyer with whom they come in contact, they are in contact with buyers. Some of the buyers they meet have no agent representation and are unaware of the importance of a home inspection. In these instances, the affiliate should have you in mind.

Save the affiliate office visits until later in your campaign, but do not ignore them.

Office Record Sheet
Whenever you meet a new agent, get his or her card and document the visit on your Agent Office Farming sheet. When you return to the office, enter the office, agent, and contact details including what you talked about in your database software.

Later, you will want to know how you met a referring agent so that you can measure your results. When your schedule begins to fill in, you will need to focus your marketing on the most effective means to target agents who appreciate your communications style. Without good records, you may be wasting valuable time, energy, and money on techniques and events that show very little return.

Local Boards of REALTORS®
The importance of joining your local Boards of REALTORS® was discussed. The benefits of joining far outweigh the costs and can lead to many long-lasting relationships. Your credibility is enhanced when agents see you attending board events.

Ask the agent who helped you prioritize your lists which board he or she belongs to and which would be most beneficial for you to start out with. For now, one membership should be enough to get you started. You can join additional boards as your business grows. If you do not have an agent friend who can help you, do an online search for "Board of REALTORS® in [your city]" or

"Association of REALTORS® in [your city]." One of these searches should lead you to the site you're looking for.

Once you are a member, you should attend the REALTOR® Marketing Sessions (RMSs). Many boards have meetings where just the affiliates get together to plan activities and events, assign responsibilities to volunteers, and network. In addition, you will find opportunities to chair or sit on committees with specific tasks, such as planning a charitable event. The cost is only your time, and you are likely to find yourself working side by side with successful, committed agents. What better way to show your professionalism and excellent communication skills?

Home Inspector Success Track—12-Week Start-Up

Week 1: Initial Office Visits

"Meet and greet" the administrative assistant in all the real estate offices in your area. Bring a small introductory gift (for example, a coffee mug filled with office supplies and goodies or a clear jar filled with candy that has your company name/logo on it). This is your first meeting, so keep it short and simple. Ask the assistant, "By the way, in the future where would be a good spot for me to leave things for the agents?" You also can consider giving a lesser gift to the other assistants, but you want to make sure the administrative assistant feels special. He or she is the key to the office.

Make sure you contact the agents whose names you wrote down with the help of your agent friend and work on your "Ten Benefits" flyer or other sales flyer that includes your USPs.

Week 2: Postcards

Deliver a "Ten Benefits" flyer to each agent's mailbox. Use the flyer from your class materials as a template to develop your own. Consider getting about 500 postcards printed.

Week 3: Deliver Brochures

Deliver a brochure to each mailbox and set up the brochure holder/candy bowls with extra brochures and business cards. The key is to put a flyer in each mailbox, and you might consider putting a gift certificate in each brochure. Fasten your card and a brochure to the holder; otherwise, other inspectors may use it.

Week 4: Postcards

Deliver a "What are customers saying" postcard to each mailbox.

Week 5: Take a Break—Do Some Passive Marketing

Call on your sphere of influence (contact database) and send thank-you notes. Take time to develop new concepts for flyers. You also can find professional home inspection flyers at www.homeinspectionflyers.com.

Look for agents who appear in the Local Board of REALTORS® newsletter or your local newspapers for accomplishments and send them a congratulatory letter with some business cards. Many agents make the top selling list at their office, which is then announced in a press release. If you see a press release or an article about an agent, clip it and send it to the agent with a personal note congratulating him or her. The agent will love you for it!

Week 6: Postcards

Develop and deliver (www.homeinspectionflyers.com) an educational postcard for agents on a topic related to home inspections. Make sure you cite the source(s) used for the article.

Week 7: Affiliate Marketing

Meet with people other than REALTORS® (for example, bankers, insurance agents, and mortgage lenders). Leave a few brochures and business cards in each office.

Begin the process again in new offices.

Week 1: (New Offices)

"Meet and greet" the administrative assistant in four to six offices. Bring a small introductory gift.

Week 8: Postcards

Deliver informational postcards about your company with a token gift (a small item—a pen or candy, for instance).

Week 2: (New Offices)

Deliver flyers to each agent's mailbox.

Week 9: Review Week

Where am I in regard to business? Are you reaching your goals? What is working? Are some offices not producing? Why? How can you meet those agents personally?

Week 3: (New Offices)

Deliver a brochure to each mailbox and set up brochure holder/candy bowl with extra brochures and business cards.

Week 10: Postcards

Deliver educational postcards.

Week 4: (New Offices)

Deliver a "What Are Customers Saying" flyer to each mailbox.

Week 11: Passive Marketing

Call on your sphere of influence, send thank-you notes, and develop concepts for articles or flyers.

Week 5: (New Offices)

Conduct passive marketing.

Week 12: "Ask for the Business" Postcards

This may be a flyer with a coupon or a hook so that agents want to work with you.

Week 6: (New Offices)

Deliver educational postcards.

Throughout these 12 weeks, you should schedule a couple of office presentations and attend several RMS sessions. Your involvement in the real estate community is establishing roots and taking hold, and fruit is appearing on the vine. Congratulations, you've successfully started your new career as a home inspector!

Keep the ball rolling and avoid the "arrival" mind-set. After arriving in this business, you must continue to commit at least eight hours a week to marketing even after you've reached your targeted goal for inspections. Inspectors who believe it's time to stop marketing watch their business begin to falter after about 60 to 90 days.

When you're green, you're *growing*.
When you're ripe, you're *rotting*.

Stay green and stay in business!

PHONE TRAINING PROGRAM

PHONE TRAINING PROGRAM OVERVIEW

Your job is to take incoming phone inquiries from customers and transform those inquiries into scheduled appointments. The success of the company rests on your ability to do just that.

These are the steps to follow in this training program:

Step 1: Accompany an inspector on an inspection before you begin answering the phone and taking inspection orders. Watch quietly and observe what is going on. Pay attention to what is being inspected. Also watch the interaction between the inspector and the customer during the inspection. This experience will be beneficial when you talk to a homebuyer about what the inspection covers, how long the inspection takes, and how to prepare for the inspection.

Step 2: You should read about home inspections and the process. In this book, spend time reading the sections on all of the types of inspections. Spend time looking over the *Property Inspection Report* to learn what's inspected.

Step 3: Accompany an inspector on a second inspection, this time paying more attention to the role of the agent and other parties at the inspection. Notice how carefully the inspector checks the house and follows the report.

Step 4: Take time to sit back and think. Imagine being in the customer's shoes— making a big investment in the purchase of a home, not being too sure what's going to happen at the inspection, having many questions, and perhaps being worried that problems with the house won't be found.

The customer goes through many emotions during a real estate transaction, and you should understand that this is the person you will be talking to on the phone.

Now imagine that you are the customer. How would you want to be treated when you called a home inspection company? What would make you feel comfortable with the company? What would convince you to make an appointment with the company?

Step 5: Learn what to expect when a customer makes an inquiry call and how to handle the call. Practice the **phone script** provided in this book. After you've practiced by yourself, find someone to role-play a call with you and try to balance following the script with meeting the needs of the customer.

Phone Training—The Scheduler's Role

A scheduler (essentially the person answering the phone) should form a relationship with each caller. And that means recognizing the caller as a person and getting to know him or her. One scheduler said that after taking 20 phone calls on a given day, she's made 20 new friends. To her, they're not strangers any longer. That's what is meant by forming a relationship on the phone.

Get the person's name at the beginning of each phone call and introduce yourself. Then keep the conversation on a first name basis. This not only reminds the customer that you're more than a voice on the other end of the line, but also personalizes the conversation and helps you focus on the relationship.

A scheduler must have an attitude of helpfulness. A *genuine* desire to serve and help the customer is easily communicated. A phony friendliness also is easily communicated, but it turns people off. So, it is critical to truly *care* about the customer. Care about the customer's new home and care that he or she gets the best home inspection service possible.

Schedulers should be themselves. Often, telemarketers develop a telephone personality that's not their own; it's too peppy or too slick. Something just doesn't ring true. You've probably been called by some of them. They're terrible, aren't they? It makes you want to hang up. Try not to let yourself become someone else when you are talking to customers.

A scheduler should be sensitive to the customer. It would be easy to teach you how to answer the phone and make appointments if all customers were alike and you could say the same thing. That's not how it works. A scheduler must *listen* to the customer, *respond* to the customer's needs, and *adjust* the conversation to fit the customer. You have to feel your way through the conversation.

You've experienced the slick telemarketer, who goes on and on without listening to a word you're saying, haven't you? It makes you wonder if he or she remembers that you're on the other end of the line. That's not the way to do it. Listen. Respond. Adjust. Be sensitive.

Phone Training—The Customer

Here are some important points to remember while you are speaking to customers on the phone.

- Most customers are shopping. That's the way the industry works. Real estate agents usually suggest three or four home inspection companies to their clients. Some clients will call these companies to compare prices, whereas others will continue to shop. In any case, callers are checking you out when they call.

- Customers may think they're shopping for price. They are, but they're also shopping for something else—whether or not they know it. They're looking for a professional company that will do an excellent job for them. They're looking for people who care about their situation and are helpful. They're looking for someone on the phone who will listen and respond to them. Customers may not know this until they call your company and find it. Then your company stands out from the rest and becomes a customer's first choice.

- Some customers call to weed out the home inspection companies they don't want. This is a very important point that is not to be forgotten. For some reason, these people think about the shopping process this way:

It's like shopping for clothes and scanning the store to eliminate areas where you know you won't find what you want. These customers will call several companies with the idea of reducing the number of contenders. So their frame of mind is to find a reason *not* to go with your company. The reasons can include having the phone answered by an answering machine, not being treated with respect on the phone, being given a price without any explanation, not being helped with questions, not being convinced that this company will do a good job for them. The list goes on. The *AHIT* approach to handling customers on the phone takes these reasons into account. You don't want to give the caller a reason to eliminate your company.

- More than half of all callers won't schedule an appointment on the first call. If you've done your job well, they'll call back. The customer may want to call other home inspection companies first or may need to discuss their choice with a spouse before making a decision. Sometimes, people call before they've made an offer to purchase the home and need to wait until the real estate transaction is further along. The *AHIT* approach takes this into account too. Everything you've been told to do in these pages is intended to make the customer remember you and the benefits of hiring your company and to call you back.

- If you push for an appointment when a customer isn't ready to make one, you won't get the appointment. When the caller is shopping, you may be first on the list of companies called. If the caller is determined to call the rest of the companies, no matter what you say, and you keep pushing to schedule an appointment now, you'll turn him or her off. You can be sure that potential customer won't call back. This is why you must be sensitive to customers. If the customer has firmly indicated that he or she will be calling other companies and doesn't want to schedule an appointment now, you need to be respectful of that fact. You should concentrate on being helpful and letting the customer know the benefits of hiring your company. If all this is done professionally, the caller will hire you.

- Many callers will be buyers. Home inspectors are hired by buyers who have made an offer to purchase a home. Although your company offers other types of inspections, the buyer inspection is your best seller. So most of your calls will be from buyers or their agents. It's important that you learn about the real estate industry and understand what the buyer is going through.

- Sometimes, the agent or broker calls to schedule an appointment for their client. He or she may have already decided to use your company, and the conversation will be short and sweet. But when the agent is shopping, you need to let him or her know some but not all of the same information you'd tell a buyer. Be selective in providing the selling points that will impress the agent as opposed to those that would impress a buyer.

Phone Training—Before the Call

Make sure you have the following items next to the phone so that you can take down information and schedule appointments.

- Several copies of blank appointment sheets. You will need to complete one for each incoming inquiry call. Make several copies for your use.

- Your company's pricing list and blank paper. As you ask questions about the property to be inspected, you'll need to write down the base price and add-ons. Later, you'll add these numbers to get a total price. If you're bad with numbers, write down the numbers on paper as you go along and use a calculator to determine the total.

- Schedule of appointments. Print out a copy of the schedule of upcoming appointments for your own use. As you make new appointments, you should add them to this schedule to prevent overbooking.

- A tally sheet. Use the tally sheet to track calls and scheduled appointments. This is important for measuring the success of your scheduling program.

Phone Training—The Incoming Call

The scheduler should be prepared to control the direction of incoming phone calls. The phone call breaks down to these five basic steps. Keep these steps in mind as you direct a customer through a call.

If the call starts with a statement such as "I need a price for a home inspection," you should tell the caller that the price depends on the property to be inspected and that you'll need to ask questions about the property so you can provide an exact price.

First find out what kind of inspection the customer wants. It is usually a buyer inspection, but you need to confirm that. Ask if the customer is buying the property. Some people will tell you that they also need a radon or mold test. Check the appropriate types of inspections on the appointment sheet.

NOTE: Do not mention the radon or mold test at this time if the customer hasn't requested a quote. This is not the time to try to sell the caller an extra service. Wait until the end of the conversation to suggest the radon or mold test.

Next, ask for the customer's name. Some callers feel uncomfortable about providing this information and don't want to give it to you. Tell the caller that you need his or her name so that you know whom the quote is for. Then if the caller doesn't schedule an appointment today, if he or she calls back, you'll have the quote ready. If the caller still refuses, try to get a first name at least. Once you know the caller's first name, use it in your conversation.

Another thing you may want to know—especially if you have inspectors working in specific areas—is the general location of the property. You may need to know the city, suburb, or side of town so that you can check a particular inspector's schedule. Ask the caller what general area the property is in. Note that some customers will be reluctant to give you any information because they're afraid you'll call and hassle them if they don't hire you. Be sensitive to this. You don't want to put any pressure on them, so don't try to get an address or phone number at this time.

Finally, ask for the property information and fill in the property section of the appointment sheet. This process is a good time to establish a friendly relationship with the customer. Be helpful and answer any questions that come up.

As you're filling in the information, keep track of the base price and the add-ons. Add them up and record the total in the "fees" section of the appointment sheet.

This is an important point during your conversation. When you state the price for the customer, *without taking a breath*, begin to talk about the home inspection. If you state the price and pause, the caller may take the opportunity to say "Thank you. That's what I wanted to know." and hang up. You do *not* want to lose the call at this point. So give the caller the price and move on.

What you're really doing when you give customers information about how the inspection will work is letting them know what's special about your company. All of these points are *benefits* and add to the customer's comfort level. Some benefits are listed here. Make sure you study the phone script for the right words to use.

- The inspection will include [explain how thorough it is] and will take approximately [number of hours].

- The customer is encouraged to follow the inspector during the inspection and is encouraged to ask questions.

- The inspection report will detail all of the inspector's findings.

- If the report contains many photos, mention that. If the report is delivered at the inspection, mention that.

- If you give a maintenance book or video with your inspections, mention that.

- If you give a 90 to 100 day inspection warranty, mention that.

When real estate agents call, you don't have to elaborate on all of these points, but you can mention a few to gain their attention.

Ask the caller if he or she has any questions about the inspection. Answer specific questions only when you know what you're talking about. It's all right to tell the customer that you don't know an answer. Just be honest. Tell the customer that an inspector can call him or her back with the answer or that you'll find the answer and call back.

With people who don't seem know much about home inspection, you may want to approach them differently. Ask if they'd like to know what the inspector will do during the inspection. Follow the phone script, but be sensitive to their responses. Pause and ask if you're providing too much information. Tell them to stop you when they've heard enough or are satisfied that your company is the right one for them.

Wording is very important during these phone calls. Don't ask if the customer wants to schedule an appointment; instead ask what day the customer would like the inspection. Quickly check your schedule for available times on that day and say, "I can schedule you for 9 or 3. Which time would be better for you?" You'll learn at this point whether the customer is ready to schedule an inspection with you. Try to get the appointment booked, but do *not* push a reluctant customer. Keep communications open so that he or she wants to call you back.

After you settle on an appointment day and time, fill in the rest of the information on the appointment sheet—both names if married, addresses, phone numbers, and agent information. Mention that your company also does radon and mold testing and ask if the customer has any concerns about these. Repeat the price you quoted for the inspection and let the customer know the fee will be collected at the site. NOTE: If you've set up a system to collect payments by credit card, this is the time to collect the payment. Tell the customer to confirm the appointment time with the agents and seller and to call you back if there's a scheduling problem with any of the parties.

NOTE: You may want to develop a system of confirming appointments with all parties involved. Doing so ensures that important information is provided to everyone involved. It is your business, so be professional and make sure everyone knows about the appointment. Agents will need to confirm with sellers, or if the house is vacant, they must make sure it is open and utilities are turned on for the inspection.

Automated services are available for inspectors that make creating schedules and confirming appointments easy to do. One such service is available at www.inspectionsupport.net. This scheduling, tracking, confirmation system works well for many inspectors. Other scheduling programs are built into software systems that are readily available for inspectors.

If you don't get the order during the first phone call, try to find out why the customer isn't ready to schedule and let that reason direct the rest of the conversation. If the customer hasn't made the offer to purchase yet or needs to talk to a spouse, you can suggest that the customer call back when he or she is ready. Then say that you want him or her to remember what sets your company apart from other home inspectors and explain your unique sales position(s) or what makes you different or special from your competition.

If the customer is going to continue shopping, acknowledge that fact. Tell the customer to keep your company in mind when talking to other home inspectors because he or she will want to hire the best. Make a final attempt at booking the appointment by suggesting that you *pencil in* a convenient time to hold the time for the customer. He or she can always call back to cancel.

In closing, remind both types of callers that you'll keep the price quote on hand so that an appointment can be scheduled quickly when they call back. Encourage them to call you back if they have any questions.

GENERAL NOTES: There are plenty of opportunities during this conversation to be helpful, interested, and caring. Be sensitive to the caller and listen carefully. You'll have to feel your way through the conversation. In general, you want to convey a feeling that you're there to help the caller. You don't want to pressure him or her into hiring your company.

The Phone Script for a Typical Home Inspection Inquiry and Booking

Below is a typical phone script. Using the same greeting and conversation each time will make this an easy process. You will develop your script to suit your company's services as well as your USPs. As your company grows, you will be able to train staff using your script, which will create uniformity.

GREETING

[Your company's name]. This is [your name]. How may I help you?

STEP 1: GETTING INFORMATION

The cost of the inspection depends on the property we're looking at. If I can ask a few questions about the property, I'll let you know exactly what the inspection will cost.

Are you buying the property? Okay. May I have your name? I'm going to write that down so that I can keep the quote on file for you.

(Optional) In what general area (city, suburb, side of town) is the property located? I don't need the exact address now.

Is this a single-family home? What style is the home? About how many square feet would you say it is [first name]? Do you know how old the home is? How many bedrooms? How many baths? Does the home have fireplaces? How many? Does it have a fireplace? Also, if the customer has the address and you are near a computer, you can take the address and visit Zillow or Realtor.com to verify the information is correct.

Does the home have a basement or a crawl space? (Basement) Is that a full basement? (Crawl space) Is that a dirt crawl space? Do you know if the crawl space has a plastic cover?

[First name], do you know how many furnaces the home has? Does it have central air-conditioning? How many water heaters? Does the property have more than one electrical service? We're almost finished. I just need to ask about the garage. Is it an attached garage? Okay. Is that a two-car garage?

Thank you. Have we covered the features of the house? Is there anything you think I've missed? Okay, that's it then.

NOTE: Before moving to the price, now is the time to tell the customer about your company, your qualifications, and ways you are different from other inspection companies.

STEP 2: PRICE AND HOME INSPECTION BENEFITS

The price of a home inspection for this property is [dollar amount]. *(Do not pause.)* This inspection will take about two to four hours [depending on the size and features]. It can take longer than that, [first name], which is good for you to know for scheduling purposes because we recommend that you be at the home inspection for your own comfort and for the information, so we can educate you on the condition of the home you are buying.

We invite you to join the inspector during the inspection. This is your service. [Your company's name] is working for you, and it's a good educational tour of the home. The inspector will tell you what's happening while he (or she) is inspecting the home and will let you know what he (or she) is finding. Of course, the inspector will answer any questions you have during the inspection.

The inspector will create the report as he (or she) goes through the home. After the inspection, the inspector will sit down with you and review each report/summary. (If you don't deliver the report on site, you should tell the customer when the report will be delivered to him or her.)

We recommend that you read the entire report from cover to cover so that you understand the inspection findings. It's a good idea to do that before you release the contingency of having the home inspected. Also, if you have any questions, you can call us back so that the inspector can clear up your questions before you close the deal.

Oh, I forgot to tell you that [your company's name] will give you a complimentary Home Maintenance Manual after the inspection. It's our gift to you.

STEP 3: QUESTIONS AND HOME INSPECTION DETAIL

Do you have any questions you'd like to ask about the inspection? I'd be happy to answer them.

(Questions you can't answer) I'm sorry, [first name], I don't know the answer to your question. I can have an inspector call you back, or I can call you back as soon as I have the answer.

(Optional) If you like, I can tell you a little more about the home inspection. Okay. Now stop me if I'm giving you too much information. Feel free to interrupt me anytime you want.

The inspector will start outside by taking a look at the exterior—the windows, caulking, siding, and foundation. He (or she) will look at the landscaping to see if there are any areas that might be causing drainage problems. The inspector will check the roof by looking at the roof covering, chimneys, flashings, gutters, and downspouts.

The inspector will look in the attic where he (or she) will check the sheathing/decking, rafters, insulation, and ventilation.

The inspector will go through the inside, checking the condition of the ceilings, floors, and walls as well as the operation of windows and doors. He (or she) will do a random testing of electrical outlets, testing all outlets near water, which can be a safety hazard. The inspector also will be watching for water problems such as leaking around showers and tubs. He (or she) will check to see that you've got adequate water pressure.

(If a basement is in the home) In the basement, the inspector will remove the front panel from the electrical box to inspect the wiring and let you know what kind of electrical service you have. The visible foundation walls will be checked for their condition. Also, the plumbing will be checked from the basement or crawl space for leaking and corroding pipes.

Well, that's a brief description of what will happen, [first name]. I can answer any specific questions you may have.

STEP 4: ASKING FOR THE APPOINTMENT

[First name], did you have a particular day in mind for the inspection?
Okay. I can schedule you for [time] or [time] on that day. Which would be better for you?

STEP 5: FINISHING UP WITH YES CALLERS

Okay. I'll put you on the schedule for [time] on [date]. What's the address of the property for the inspection? And your present address? I'll need your home and work numbers in case I need to call you before the inspection. Thank you. Can you give me the name of the agent you're working with? That's the agent who's representing you, right? Do you have his (or her) phone number? Great. What real estate company is he (or she) with? Okay.

Can you tell me how you heard about our company? (Always track this.)

I should mention, [first name], that we also do radon and mold testing if you need them. Would you like to know about those services?

(Optional) [Your company's name] follows the EPA standards for radon and mold testing, and the EPA recommends that we place two detectors at the site. We use charcoal canisters or continuous radon monitor, which is the most accurate short-term test available and is recognized by all relocation companies. By short-term, I mean that we have to leave the monitor in place for only 48 hours to get accurate results. The long-term tests can take several days or weeks. After the monitor is picked up, you will have your results immediately. We'll tell you the level of radon gas in the home and explain what that means. I can have the inspector perform the test if you wish. The cost would be [dollar amount].

Now before I let you go, let me confirm the price I gave you. That's [dollar amount] for the home inspection. That fee will be collected at the inspection site. Let them know what form of payments you accept.

We'll see you on [date] at [time]. You should call your agent and confirm that the appointment works for him (or her) and the seller. If you need to change the appointment, give me a call. If I don't hear from you, I'll assume that everything's all right. I'll call you the day before your inspection to remind you of your appointment.

STEP 5: FINISHING UP WITH "NOT NOW" CALLERS

You're not ready to schedule an appointment yet?

- *(Talk to spouse)* Of course. You'll certainly want to do that, although I could pencil in an appointment to reserve a time for you. You can always cancel it.

- *(No offer yet)* Oh, I see. Well, I hope you'll call me back after you make the offer to purchase. And good luck with the house.

- *(Still shopping)* That's all right. I know you're looking for the best home inspection service.

I'd like to tell you what sets our home inspection company apart from other home inspection companies so that you'll remember us. First, you should know that our highly skilled inspectors must meet and abide by state and national standards and a code of ethics. There are several national associations for inspectors. One is ASHI, the national professional organization that serious home inspection companies join. *(If true)* Our company is an ASHI member, of course, and so are our inspectors. Also, our inspectors are certified by the American Home Inspectors Training Institute, which is an ASHI-affiliated school. We're serious about having the best inspectors.

Another thing that sets us apart is that we're fully insured. We have errors and omissions insurance as well as liability and workmen's comp. That's important for you to know in case anything goes wrong.

The best in inspector training and full insurance coverage are two areas in which some companies cut corners because of the expense. But remember that [your company's name] has both.

I'll keep your price quote on hand, [first name], so that when you call back, we can set up an appointment right away. And listen. Please call me back if you have any questions or I can help you in any way.

Evaluating Performance

Success on the phone is judged by how many appointments the scheduler can make. You can grade that performance with the close rate, which is expressed as a percentage. It tells you what percent of incoming inquiry calls turn into appointments.

AHIT's experience is that a scheduler can achieve a very good close rate of nearly 80%. That means that if 10 calls come in, 7 or 8 of them become appointments. But remember, over half of first calls don't result in booked appointments. Many appointments are booked when the customer calls the second time. So the total of appointments from first and second calls is 80% of all incoming calls.

Another statistic you should know is that about 10% of appointments already made are canceled. Cancellations are most likely not the fault of the scheduler. Instead, it's due to the nature of the real estate business, where buyers can change their minds about houses and do not need the inspection any longer.

Schedulers should use a tally sheet to keep a record of all incoming inquiry calls, calls that turn into appointments on the first call and second call, and appointments that are canceled. The scheduler can make tic marks to record calls and appointments and count them at the end of the time period (at the end of the week, for example). Then he or she can calculate percentages. (For instance, the percentage of first-call appointments is the number of those calls divided by the total number of incoming calls.) The close rate is the sum of first-call and second-call appointment percentages. The scheduler can follow a weekly close rate and even use the totals to calculate a close rate over longer periods of time. He or she should set goals and strive to improve the close rate each week.

A scheduler also should evaluate the length of each incoming call. There's a lot of information to cover with each customer, and at first, the calls may run long. But as the scheduler gains more experience, he or she should be able to close an appointment in 10 or 15 minutes.

REVIEW INSPECTION SALES PROGRAM

A review inspection is sold to a buyer of a property when your company has performed the original seller inspection (commonly called a listing inspection). It's a walk-through inspection performed for the buyer by the same inspector and using the seller's copy of the original *Property Inspection Report*. This inspection will take about half the time of the original seller's inspection (usually about an hour).

The sale of a review inspection is not automatic. The steps used to get this sale are as follows:

1. The inspector speaks with the seller and agent at the site and asks them to put the buyer in touch with the inspector's company, either by calling in the buyer's name and phone number or by having the buyer call in.

2. Follow-up letters are sent to the seller and the agent, reminding them to pass along the buyer's name.

3. When the inspection company receives the buyer's name and phone number from the seller or agent (or the buyer calls the office), the scheduler calls the buyer to sell the review inspection.

At the Seller Inspection

When the inspector finishes a seller inspection, he or she should introduce the idea of a review inspection to the seller and the real estate agent. The inspector's goal is to get the seller and/or the agent to realize that suggesting the review inspection to the buyer benefits them too.

The inspector can present the ideas using these steps:

1. Tell the seller and agent about the review inspection—that it's a walk-through where you reinspect the property using the original inspection report. You look over the property again and note fixes or replacements, talk about the findings with the buyer, and answer any questions.

2. Explain to the seller and agent the benefits for *them*. Explain that turning over the report and bringing back an inspector familiar with the property contributes to the buyer's comfort level on disclosure issues. They can reduce the time it will take a buyer to shop for another home inspector and will sell the home faster.

3. Explain to the seller and agent the benefits to the *buyer*. Explain that a review inspection will save them money because it's less than half the price of a full inspection. They get to see the original report, and the inspector reinspects everything with them and notes improvements. They can ask questions, and your inspection company will give them a Home Maintenance Manual.

4. Ask the seller and/or agent to put the buyer in touch with you for the purpose of scheduling a review inspection with the buyer.

Following is a short script for the inspector to use. It's not meant to be memorized and given in a particular way, but it may be helpful in knowing how to lead into the subject.

Inspector Script: REVIEW INSPECTION

When you find a buyer for the home, call me back. We offer a review inspection that the buyer can hire us to do. I'll come back to reinspect everything so that the buyer is comfortable with the inspection report we just finished. I'll walk the buyer through the house and talk about the findings. It will take about half the time we took today.

I'll use your copy of the report for the walk-through. Buyers like that because they can see the report and it shows that you have nothing to hide. Then if you fix some of the things I found today or replace anything, I can let the buyer know. And I can mark that improvement on the report.

SELLER AND AGENT BENEFITS

You made a good decision to have the home inspected before you showed it. It's a good preventative measure as far as liability is concerned. And I know it's a good selling point with buyers. They're attracted to a home that's already had a home inspection. But you might use the review inspection to help you even more. If you tell buyers that you'll turn over the original inspection report and have me come back to review it with them, they'll relax on disclosure issues. Also, you can reduce the time it takes the buyer to shop for another home inspector and can close the deal faster.

BUYER BENEFITS

A review inspection is a good deal for a buyer too. And you might want to let him or her know this. The cost to the buyer is less than half of what he or she would pay for a brand new home inspection. We'd charge only [percentage of the original price or flat fee], so the buyer can save money. Of course, you would need to assure the buyer that [your company's name] performs a fair and impartial inspection. The buyer would want to know that.

The benefit to the buyer is that he or she gets a complete walk-through of the property with an inspector who is already familiar with it. And the buyer gets to see your original report with everything disclosed and see the improvements you made. That contributes to his or her comfort level. Of course, the buyer will be able to ask me any questions he or she has about the findings. I'll take whatever time is necessary to talk with the buyer.

You also can tell the buyer that I'll be giving him or her a Home Maintenance Manual as a gift. [Your company's name] does that for all buyers. The Home Maintenance Manual teaches the buyer how to perform a step-by-step checkup on the home every six months. But it goes beyond simple home repair; it shows the buyer what danger signs to watch for before they get out of hand.

GETTING THE COMMITMENT

I'm going to leave an extra brochure and business card with you for the buyer. Could you call me when a buyer makes an offer to purchase? Just let me know the buyer's name and phone number, and I'll contact him or her to set up an appointment. You could have the buyer call our office, but if you give me the name and number, I can handle it and make it easier for the buyer. Of course, you will need to assure the buyer that [your company's name] performs a fair and impartial inspection. The buyer will want to know that.

Follow-up

When the inspector returns to the office after the seller inspection, the post inspection form should be marked for follow-up letters to be sent to both the seller and the agent. These letters will remind both parties about the review inspection and to pass on the buyer's name to you.

Selling the Buyer

If a buyer has been informed of the review inspection by the seller or agent, he or she may call the office directly to schedule an appointment. If your pricing scheme sets the price of the review inspection as a percentage of the seller inspection, the scheduler would have to find that information in the seller's file or in the customer database before quoting a price for the review inspection.

> What is more likely to happen is that the seller or the agent will let your office know the name and phone number of the buyer. In that case, the scheduler should call the buyer and try to sell the review over the phone.

Before making the phone call, the scheduler should retrieve the seller's file and make sure the original appointment sheet is handy. This sheet contains a great deal of information that the scheduler won't have to collect again. The price of the review inspection can be calculated before the scheduler calls. A new appointment sheet should be completed for the review inspection.

A script is provided for the scheduler to follow when making this outgoing phone call. The scheduler should be aware that the buyer has probably heard about your company from the seller or the agent and may know quite a bit about the review inspection. But the buyer may feel uneasy about the seller suggesting the home inspector.

The scheduler should let the buyer know that this is a normal arrangement with the company—that is, to do a seller inspection and then follow up with a review inspection for the buyer. It's also important to let the buyer know that your company is **an impartial third party** to the transaction. Buyers may be a little suspicious that your company is somehow in the REALTORS® or seller's pocket on this deal. Address the issue directly as the script suggests and let them know that your inspection company operates by a strict code of ethics.

Follow these basic steps with the phone call:

- In the greeting, let the buyer know who gave you his or her name and why you called.

- Discuss what a review inspection is and mention the price. *Without taking a breath*, move on to the benefits of the review inspection, which are as follows:

    —The review inspection is less than half the price of a new inspection.

    —The customer will receive the seller's copy of the original inspection report and be able to take it home after the review inspection.

    —The inspector will reinspect everything and note any changes and improvements.

    —The customer will accompany the inspector during the inspection and is encouraged to ask questions.

—The inspector will review the report with the buyer.

—The buyer will receive a complimentary Home Maintenance Manual.

- Ask if the buyer if he or she has any questions about the review inspection, but do *not* reveal any specific information from the seller's inspection report. At this point, that information is confidential to the seller.

- Assure the buyer of your company's impartiality in the real estate transaction.

- Ask for the appointment.

- Closing the conversation. (See the incoming phone call script for instructions.)

Scheduler Script—Review Inspection

GREETING

Mr. (or Mrs. or Ms.) [last name]? This is [your name] from [your company's name]. We recently did the home inspection on the property at [home address]. [Seller's or agent's name] asked me to call you about the inspection. He (or she) said that you might be interested in having us come back to the property to reinspect it for you and explain the findings from the first inspection.

REVIEW INSPECTION PRICE AND BENEFITS

After [your company's name] does an inspection for a seller, we often go back and reinspect the property for the buyer. It's called our review inspection. We offer the review inspection at less than half the price of the original home inspection. That's because we're already familiar with the property and have the report on file.

Let's see. [Seller's name] paid [dollar amount] for the original inspection. That's about what you'd pay if you hired someone else to do a new inspection. If we were to do the reinspection, the price would be [dollar amount]. *(Do not pause.)* The review inspection will take about an hour, which you may find helpful to know because we recommend that you be there to make sure you're comfortable with the inspection.

The inspector will meet you at the property and will have the seller sign the original report over to you. Then we invite you to accompany the inspector and watch as he (or she) reinspects the house. It's a good educational tour for you because the inspector will tell you what's happening while he (or she) is rechecking everything. The inspector will pay particular attention to any condition that has changed or been improved since the first inspection and note it on the report. Of course, you can ask whatever questions you have. The inspector will take the necessary time to explain things.

After the inspection, the inspector will review the report with you. It's a comprehensive report. We recommend that buyers read the report after they get home to make sure they understand the findings. That way you can call us back with any questions before you close the deal.

With a home inspection, [your company's name] gives new buyers a complimentary Home Maintenance Manual. It's our gift to you. It shows you how to perform a step-by-step checkup of your home every six months. It shows you how to watch for danger signs before they get out of hand.

QUESTIONS

Do you have any questions you'd like to ask about the review inspection? I'd be happy to answer them.

(If buyer asks specific questions about findings in the original inspection) I'm sorry I can't answer that, [first name]. The information in the inspection report is confidential to [seller's name], and we honor that confidentiality—just like we'll protect your confidentiality when the report is passed on to you. Of course, at the review inspection, you'll get to read the report for yourself and ask the inspector any questions you have.

ASSURANCE OF IMPARTIAL WORK

You might be concerned about having the same inspector as [seller's name] did. First, we think it's a plus to have the home inspected by someone who is familiar with it. But I'd like to assure you that [your company's name] is an impartial third party to the real estate transaction. We don't inspect properties for the benefit of any special party. Our inspectors are technicians who simply report what they find, not what someone wants to hear. And they abide by a strict professional code of ethics and standards of practice. When we conduct the review inspection, we'll be working for you, not the seller or the agent.

ASK FOR THE APPOINTMENT

Do you know how soon you'll need the inspection? Okay. I can schedule you for [time] or [time] on [day]. Which time would be better for you?

THE HOME PRESERVATION/MAINTENANCE PLAN SALES PROGRAM

The Home Preservation/Maintenance Plan is one of *AHIT's* products that you may choose to offer. This product represents an opportunity to sell additional home inspections to your existing customers.

The Home Preservation/Maintenance Plan is sold to a customer of a **buyer inspection or review inspection** in the weeks following the inspection. It's a five-year plan in which members can purchase up to five home inspections at a fixed price.

The sale of the Home Preservation/Maintenance Plan begins at the inspection site and continues over time. The sales program used to promote this sale consists of three basic steps:

1. The inspector introduces the concept of the Home Preservation/Maintenance Plan to the customer at the inspection site.

2. A follow-up promotional letter is sent to the customer after the buyer has moved into the new home.

3. The scheduler may make a follow-up telephone call in an attempt to sell the Plan over the phone. This can call be made after the letter has been sent or can be used instead of the letter.

The Plan Concept

The Home Preservation/Maintenance Plan is a unique product. It's a new concept designed to open up a new market for your home inspection business. On your part, it makes good marketing sense to have additional products to sell to customers who have purchased your good services. On the part of the new homeowner, it makes sense to take steps to protect the value of the investment in a new home.

Home Preservation/Maintenance, as *AHIT* uses the term, is a **program of ongoing home inspections** after the home is purchased. Home Preservation/Maintenance is the task of checking out all the components of a home on a regular basis to catch problems before they get out of hand. The term *Home Preservation/Maintenance* is used because the concept of ongoing checkups goes beyond home repair and home maintenance, which are measures taken *after* things go wrong with a home. Home Preservation/Maintenance is a program of the steps taken periodically to monitor the condition of a home to *prevent* things from going wrong.

Home Preservation/Maintenance is like preventive medicine. It's like going to the doctor for an annual physical to find out what's in good condition, what needs some monitoring, and what's needed to keep the body in shape. The same is true for a home.

For specific reasons, a big deal is made out of using the words *Home Preservation/Maintenance* in talking about the booklet, and the Plan. The terms *home repair* and *home maintenance* are tired words that have been around a while. They conjure up an image of the homeowner repairing a leaky faucet. Home Preservation/Maintenance can be a larger concept.

The Home Maintenance Manual and the Plan are part of the home preservation concept. They are related in important ways:

- The booklet lets the homeowner keep track of the items that are being preserved. It allows the homeowner to build a Home History file so that when the homeowner sells his or her home, it is prepared to market in good condition.

- The Home Preservation/Maintenance Plan is a program the homeowner can join to have these checkups done professionally. The Plan offers homeowners up to five home inspections at a fixed price that will hold over a five-year period. The Plan is a program of ongoing home inspections performed by professional home inspectors. It's designed for homeowners who feel less than confident about performing the checkups on their own.

AHIT's customer marketing plan purposefully connects the free Home Maintenance Manual and home preservation booklet to the Home Preservation/Maintenance Plan in both concept and visual design. Giving the manual as a gift to buyers is a lead-in to selling the Home Preservation/Maintenance Plan—and in time, selling Home Preservation/Maintenance Inspections to these customers.

The Terms

The terms of the Home Preservation/Maintenance Plan are simple and easily communicated. Here is an explanation of the terms and suggestions for setting your company's prices of the Plan.

- The buyer pays a membership fee to join. This fee is paid when the buyer joins the Plan. It's a nonrefundable fee and is not meant to be applied against the cost of an inspection the member may purchase under the Plan.

  AHIT suggests about *$50 to $75* for this upfront membership fee. If you offer this optional product, you will need to set your own fee. You should keep it reasonable and not make the price an obstacle in selling the Plan.

  Membership lasts five years. It starts the day the customer joins the Plan and ends on the anniversary date five years later. For example, if a customer joins the Plan on June 10, 2015, the membership ends on June 10, 2020.

- During the five years the member is in the Plan, he or she can purchase up to five Home Preservation/Maintenance Inspections from your company. Actually, five is the limit, but the member has no obligation to buy any. The member will decide when to have the inspections. Each inspection purchased under the Plan is the same thorough home inspection you normally provide with the Property Inspection Report. Nothing is different, and there are no shortcuts.

  Members of the Home Preservation/Maintenance Plan should be allowed to purchase these five inspections on their home for *any* reason. At some time in the future, they may decide to sell their home and want a seller inspection. They may even want to purchase a buyer inspection on a new home under the Plan. It's not worth the hassle of arguing with them that the original intent of the Plan was meant for home preservation and not for other inspections. It will just alienate the member, and you'll lose the business. So once someone joins the Plan, *for whatever reason*, you should let them purchase up to five inspections at the price you've given them.

- The inspection price remains the same during the Plan. Plan members pay a fixed price, determined when they join, for each inspection purchased over the next five years. This price varies from customer to customer depending on the price just paid for an inspection. The price is based on the current inspection price minus a small amount. One suggestion is to subtract $25 from the current inspection price. For example, if you just performed an inspection for $325, the fixed price for the Plan would be $300.

  NOTE: If you're selling the Plan to the buyer at a review inspection, the fixed price should be figured out based on the price of the seller inspection, not the review inspection price.

- The customer signs a Plan agreement. The Plan customer will sign a Home Preservation/Maintenance Plan agreement that states the membership fee, the date the customer joined the plan, and the fixed price for any inspection the customer purchases over the next five years.

When Not To Sell

The Home Preservation/Maintenance Plan needs to be sold in a series of steps. It's introduced at the buyer and review inspection to new buyers and then followed up with a letter and a phone call if necessary.

AHIT suggests that you *not* try to close the sale of the Plan at the inspection. It would be convenient to do so and you'd certainly increase your sales, but it's not a good idea. Agents often resent a home inspection company pushing for the sale of products after the inspection and can become angry. You want to avoid any trouble with agents.

NOTE: Over time, you may discover how to get past this problem of not being able to sell the Plan at the inspection. Perhaps you'll figure out how to get agents to accept it.

At the Inspection

The inspector plays an important role before, during, and after the buyer and review inspections by introducing the buyer to the concept of the Home Preservation/Maintenance Plan. The inspector's goal is to make sure the buyer understands what the Plan is and what the terms of the Plan are. The inspector also wants to generate enough interest in the Plan that buyers will remember it when they are contacted at a later date.

The inspector can present the Plan using these steps:

- Introduce the concept of home preservation. When you are having the customer sign the Preinspection Agreement before the inspection, mention that you'll be giving him or her a *Home Preservation* Home Maintenance Manual as a gift.

- Casually insert the subject of the Home Preservation Plan into the conversation during the inspection. For example, if you find something in the home that may become a problem, you can mention to the buyer that you can come back to check on it and that you'll tell him or her about a special plan to do this after the inspection.

- Talk about the terms of the Plan after the inspection. You can introduce this subject while you are reviewing the inspection report with the customer. Mention that the buyer can purchase up to five home inspections over the next five years at a fixed price.

- Explain the benefits of the Plan. Explain that it protects buyers' homes and protects the buyer from rising home inspection costs. Explain that the customer gets professional assistance in taking care of the home. State the fixed price for inspections under the Plan.

- Give the customer a Home Preservation/Maintenance Inspection brochure and Plan promotional items.

A short script starts on the following page. It's to be used only as a guide. The script isn't meant to be memorized. But it may be helpful in knowing how to lead into the subject of the Home Preservation/Maintenance Plan.

Inspectors will have to play this by ear. You don't want to seem to be making a sales pitch in front of the agent, and yet you want to let customers know about the Plan. You can easily make comments to the customer before and during the inspection. It's the introduction of the details at the end of the inspection that takes a little more time. Generally, the agent will not be standing around when you review the report with the buyer, so you'll have a chance then to talk about the Plan and give the customer the promotional items.

CAUTION: You are not trying to close a sale at the inspection. You are simply introducing the Plan. So don't take too much time talking about the Plan with the buyer. This is not a full-fledged sales pitch. And don't be pushy about it. This is a soft sell. Remember too that the agent will not be happy if you taking time trying to sell the customer something else.

Inspector Script for Home Preservation/Maintenance Plan

Use this script only as a guide. It isn't meant to be memorized and given word for word. But it may offer ideas about how to introduce the Plan at the inspection.

BEFORE THE INSPECTION

I'm going to give you a complimentary Home Maintenance Manual booklet after the inspection. It's about home preservation—something you'll want to think about after you buy the home. The video will show you how to do a step-by-step checkup of your new home, and the booklet will allow you to keep a record of what you are doing, just like I'm going to do it today.

DURING THE INSPECTION

(Make the following comments when you find something that may become a problem, such as the roof, the furnace, a basement crack, or anything of that sort, especially deferred cost items.)

(For example) The manual I'm going to give you shows you how to keep an eye on this. We offer a special Home Preservation/Maintenance Plan where we can come back to inspect this for you. We'd check everything out again.

(Or) We can come back for a checkup inspection if you want and help you keep an eye on this. That's part of our Home Preservation/Maintenance Plan.

(Or) Our complimentary manual tells you how to watch for potential problems. We can come back to inspect the house again and look for anything you're afraid you'll overlook. Our Home Preservation/Maintenance Plan will be a big help.

AFTER THE INSPECTION

Here's a gift from [your company's name]. *(Give a Home Maintenance Manual to the buyer.)* Be sure to take a look at it. It shows you how to do a step-by-step checkup of your home. For best results, we suggest a program of home checkups. That way you find anything that could turn into a problem later on.

You can always have me come back to inspect your home to make sure you're doing the checkup correctly. I'd be glad to help you.

THE PLAN

In fact, our Home Preservation/Maintenance Plan does that for you. You can have us back on a regular basis to perform professional inspections.

By joining our plan, you can purchase up to five inspections on your home over the next five years. But there's no obligation. You decide how many you want and when you want them. If you want me to come back and do an inspection every two years, that's okay.

A good part of the Plan is that we'll hold the inspection price for five years. In fact, I'll fix the price at [dollar amount] less than the full inspection cost on this home. So even if you ordered an inspection in 2020, the price would be much less.

The Plan would give you two kinds of protection. First, you'd receive repeat inspections and be alerted about any problems that come up. Second, you'd be receiving price protection. I don't know how much an inspection will cost five years from now, but it's sure to be more than it is today.

Plan members receive a free Home History file for storing home records and inspection reports. People like this because if they decide to sell, they have a complete history of the house. Buyers are impressed to learn that professional inspections have been done on a regular basis.

Here is some information about the Plan. *(Give brochure and promotional items to the buyer.)* Take some time to think about the Plan and to get settled here. Then if you decide to join, just let us know.

PROMOTIONAL LETTER/EMAIL

When the inspector returns to the office after a buyer or review inspection, the post inspection form should be marked for a standard thank-you letter/email to be sent to the customer of these inspections. This letter/email is intended to thank the customer for his or her business.

Promotional letters/emails that promote the sale of the Plan can be sent out monthly to the whole group of buyers. The post inspection form does not have to be marked for this purpose. Information about whom to send the letter/email to will be pulled from the customer database.

You should let a month pass before you send out this promotion letter/email. Give the buyers a chance to move into their new homes before you remind them of the Plan. Thus, at the end of each month when you send out these letters/emails, you'll be choosing customers not from this month, but from the month *before.*

Telephone Sales

Your company may want to try telemarketing to get previous customers of buyer and review inspections to purchase the Home Preservation/Maintenance Plan. The scheduler should make these calls. If calling turns out to be more successful than sending the letters/emails, you should stick with telemarketing.

After sending the letters/emails, let a week or so go by before you make any follow-up calls. If you want to try just telemarketing, like the promotional letters/emails, give the buyers a month or so before you call to remind them of the Plan. Toward the end of each month then, you will be calling customers not from this month, but from the month before.

NOTE: Make sure you delete names of any customers who made complaint calls about their inspection. It's not a good idea to make a promotional call to anyone who's unhappy with the inspection your company did.

The scheduler should keep this phone call short. The purpose of the call is to re-interest the buyer in the Plan and encourage him or her to join. Here are the highlights of the call:

- In the greeting, the scheduler should let the buyer know that the inspector asked him or her to call. Then the scheduler should use the video to lead into a discussion of the Plan.

- The scheduler should define what the Home Preservation/Maintenance Plan is and remind the customer that the inspector had mentioned a fixed price of inspections under the Plan.

- The scheduler should work the benefits into the conversation. He or she should explain that the Plan protects the buyer's home and protects the buyer from rising home inspection prices. The scheduler should explain that the buyer gets professional assistance in taking care of his or her home and receives a free Home History File.

- The scheduler ends the call by closing the sale or offering to send more information about the Plan to customers who are undecided about joining now.

Scheduler Script: The Home Preservation/Maintenance Plan

GREETING

Mr. (or Mrs. or Ms.) [last name]? This is [your name] from [your company's name]. We did the home inspection for you recently. Your inspector, [inspector's name], asked me to give you a call. I hope you're enjoying your new home? That's great. Are you settled in?

We recommend that you do the checkup every six months to watch for potential problems. [Your company's name] suggests regular home checkups for the best results in home preservation/maintenance. That way you find anything that may turn into a problem later on. [Inspector's name] said to remind you that he (or she) can always come back if you need help with the checkups. He (or she) would be glad to help.

HOME PRESERVATION/MAINTENANCE PLAN

[Inspector's name] told you about our Home Preservation Plan, didn't he (or she)?

With the Home Preservation Plan, we come back on a regular basis to perform professional home inspections for you. Most people like the idea of having us come back because they know they'll be able to keep their homes in good shape that way. It helps them catch problems before they get out of hand.

Some people do their own checkups. But others who worry they may overlook something ask us to give a professional opinion. That's why we developed the Home Preservation Plan—for people who want the best inspections they can get.

THE TERMS

The Plan lets you buy up to five home inspections during the five years you're a Plan member. But you're not obligated to buy a particular number of inspections. That's your decision. If you wanted your house to be inspected every two years, that would be all right. And if you remember, [inspector's name] gave you a fixed price for those inspections that we'll hold for five years.

That price was [dollar amount] less than the price of the original inspection. And we hold that price even if you order a home inspection in five years. And who knows how much an inspection will cost then. It costs you only [dollar amount] to join the Plan, and you get our Home History File when you join. That's a special file for storing all your home records and inspection reports.

Do you have any questions about the Plan that I can answer?

I want to remind you that under the Plan, you can have up to five inspections on your home. That includes an inspection in case you decide to sell and even the inspection on a new home you may be considering. [Inspector's name] may not have told you that.

CLOSING

Can I sign you up for the Plan now?

(Yes) Fine. I'll send you the Plan agreement to sign. You can return it to us along with your membership check. I'll send out your Home History File when I receive the agreement. Thanks so much.

(Don't know) I understand. Here's what I'll do. I'll send you a Plan agreement for your information. You can read it and think about it. If you have any questions, give me a call. I'll be happy to answer them. You won't be obligated in any way, but you may decide to join later. Thanks again, Mr. (or Mrs. or Ms.) [last name]. I hope to hear from you soon.

(Definitely not) Okay. Would you like me to send you information on the Plan so that you can think about it? You can always join later. Thanks so much for letting me talk to you today, Mr. (or Mrs. or Ms.) [last name].

After Selling the Plan

When a customer joins the Home Preservation/Maintenance Plan, you send out a Plan agreement. (The fixed price and other information should be filled in before it is sent out.) The customer signs and returns the agreement, enclosing a check for the membership fee. As soon as the agreement and check are received, the following must be done:

- The receipt information on the Home Preservation/Maintenance Plan agreement is filled in, signed and dated.

  The card that goes in the pocket of the Home History File is filled in, including the expiration date and the customer's fixed inspection price.

- The letter, the customer's copy of the agreement, and the Home History File are sent.

The Home Preservation Inspection

Once a customer has become a member of the Home Preservation Plan, the next step is to encourage the member to purchase inspections under the Plan. Your office should send each member a reminder letter on his or her anniversary date. If the agent purchased the Plan for his or her buyers or sellers, their names should be included on all mailings.

TAKING THE HOME INSPECTION CALLS

The Basics

This manual has covered a lot of ground so far. If you've been following the plan provided, at this point in your business, the phones should be ringing at least a few times a week with prospective clients and agents inquiring about booking an inspection.

Your referral-based marketing should be beginning to fill your contact database, and you should be becoming a presence in the real estate community. If the phone isn't ringing as often as you'd like, go out and do more marketing, and *don't get discouraged*. In this business, referral-based marketing will get the phone ringing, with volume increasing over time.

This is where your technical and communications skills come into play. Referral-based marketing gets a handful of agents and clients to call. As an example, assume that ten agents call in a two-week period and five of them book an inspection with your firm.

Once you've performed a great home inspection, an agent will be comfortable in calling you again, even if only as a backup inspector for when his or her primary inspector is unavailable. It is better to be a backup and do some of an agent's inspections than none at all. So continue with the marketing, and eventually something is likely to happen with an agent's primary inspector, at which point you will move into first place.

The main point here is with regard to service, people share their good experiences with people they know—as many as six or seven people during the year after the experience. If this is the case, 5 agents who had a positive experience with you could be referring you to as many as 35 other agents or clients. Multiply this by even more referrals and you will see how powerful this can be for your business. Try to make each person you work for your cheerleader. Your primary goals for every call re to provide excellent service, make a positive lasting impression, and maximize your opportunity for inspection referrals.

Up to this point, you've learned how to share the knowledge about your business and the value you bring to the table and how to get agents to feel good about you. Now it's time to learn ways to accomplish the same thing over the phone and to close the sale.

Who Will Call?

Many home inspectors believe they get a good mix of clients and agents calling to schedule appointments. As a professional, you should treat every first-time caller the same way.

As simple as it sounds, always answer the phone, and regardless of who is calling, use a positive, enthusiastic tone of voice. First-time callers should be taken through the educational and rapport-building processes. Continue building rapport with agents every time they call. If you don't remember an agent or the gist of your last discussion, refer to your database to review your notes. Keeping notes on every agent and every call will be a useful tool in time. You want to build long-lasting relationships by showing a sincere interest in *all* of your customers.

When an agent first calls, it usually means he or she liked something about you but will keep a close eye on you until he or she is more comfortable with your skills. Over time, you are likely to find agents working with you on a regular basis. They will be calling to book the inspection for their buyers. Congratulations! You have a well-established relationship of trust with that agent, and as long as you continue to manage the relationship, he or she will continue to call.

Preparing to Take the Calls

IMPORTANT: Answering the phone makes or breaks a home inspection business. If you do not answer your phone (or have it answered when you are doing inspections), you will not succeed in the inspection profession. This is worth repeating: *Answer your phone or don't start this business.* If you cannot answer your phone every time it rings, you should hire a service such as American's Call Center, which will pay for itself very quickly.

Before the phone rings, you must be prepared so that the call is no longer than it should be or that there are uncomfortable pauses. This is easily perceived as a lack of confidence and ability on your part and diminishes your chances of booking an appointment.

Have Your Supplies Ready

At the start of each day, turn on your computer and have your scheduling program (for example, Inspectit) open and ready to access on a moment's notice.

To avoid sounding unsure, be clear about your company's fees and other pertinent information before you begin marketing. The call should have a smooth flow and be effortless for the caller.

Make sure you have plenty of appointment sheets, your inspection calendar, and your price list on the desk next to the phone. If you use a scheduling program such as ISN, www.inspectionsupport.net, have it open and ready to use.

Finally, create a tally sheet to track the call volume and keep track of your sources. This information can also be tracked in the ISN system. A source is an advertising or marketing effort that prompted someone to call your business. Tracking these referrals may seem insignificant while you're on a call, but tallying up the results later quickly reveals your most effective marketing efforts.

If you use InspectIt, it has a method for tracking your referrals. Input this data so that you can call up reports on a regular basis and review the results of your efforts.

Taking Calls in the Field

Answering the phone, taking orders, and entering client data can be a challenge in the field. In the beginning, you may want to hire someone part-time or use a call center while you are doing inspections so that you can concentrate on that work. If you must answer the phone during an inspection, be aware that this can be a distraction from your work as well as an imposition on your client's time. Although some systems work in the field, make sure you can sync the information to your office computer.

Most home inspectors maintain a consistent backup procedure on a separate computer or on an external hard drive back at the office. It avoids the risk of losing all data if their laptop is damaged while they are out in the field.

Some inspectors have an assistant or a scheduler taking calls in the office. If you don't, you should carry a supply of appointment sheets, a hard copy of the inspection calendar, and a price sheet in the inspection vehicle at all times. So if the Internet is not available and the inspector must book an inspection from the field or the inspector's laptop/tablet or iPad is damaged, you can still do so.

Always be prepared to take an appointment call and book an inspection no matter where you are or what you are doing. But again be aware that if you are on a home inspection and your client is with you this does impose on your clients time so we highly recommend using a call service while you are performing an inspection. If your car has signs on it, someone may approach you to ask you a technical question or even schedule an inspection.

An AHIT graduate recently dropped his son off at school when another parent approached him with questions about a home inspection. The woman was buying a new spec home that was move-in ready and thought she should have it inspected. The inspector educated her on the importance of having a home inspected regardless of age. He built rapport by asking questions about the property and the neighborhood, and because he had all the necessary materials with him, he offered to book the inspection there in the school parking lot. As a result, the customer commented on his professionalism, and even though her agent had given her three other companies to call, she booked the inspection *for that afternoon*.

It pays to be prepared, so have a supply of materials with you at all times.

Manual or Web-Based?

In addition to InspectIt, AHIT offers state-of-the-art websites with an additional service that allows a customer to request a tentative inspection online after hours. People expect you to have an up-to-date website. They are looking for solutions and answers to their questions. The more solution-based functionality your website provides, the more likely you are to book an inspection.

A typical situation involves a buyer who's been given the names of three inspection firms to call but can't get to the phone until after business hours. Two home inspectors have websites, and one does not. So two of them already have an advantage over the third.

When the buyer visits the first website, he or she finds a good amount of useful information regarding the scope of an inspection, SOPs, inspector experience, and a few photos from past inspections.

Visiting the second website, the buyer finds the same useful information with an additional feature not found on the first site. The buyer finds a form to complete asking for basic information about the property, such as square footage, age, city, and the major cross streets. In addition, the buyer finds a field in which to input his or her first and second choices for inspection dates and his or her preference for a morning or afternoon inspection.

When the buyer completes this form, in his or her mind, he or she has already committed to booking an inspection. All the inspector has to do now is work up the fee based on the information the buyer provided and call the buyer back.

This is another example of providing superior customer service and unmatched professionalism. By calling the buyer back right away, you gain an edge on the competition even if the only advantage is time. More likely, the superior service makes a better impression on the buyer, giving him or her, a reason to call back for the appointment even after speaking with the other two firms. You have the potential to create a complete online order and schedule system for clients.

Investing in technology may not be in your budget right away, but you should keep it in mind when your business is growing and you need more ways for clients to book inspections. Investing in technology is a smart move as long as it serves a useful purpose by adding value to the firm and driving more business through the door.

Scheduling in Person Is Best

Having a live person who is trained to build rapport with customers and take them through the appropriate steps is still the best way to take calls. Most multi-inspector firms have a full-time assistant to do this along with other administrative duties. This is a relationship-based business that relies on referral marketing, and answering the phones in person reinforces the message of professionalism and dedication sent as part of your marketing efforts.

Some inspectors choose to maximize their first year's revenues by taking calls and scheduling the inspections personally even if it means allowing the calls to go to voice mail. If you choose to do this, you should use voice mail as was described earlier in the discussion of Web-based scheduling. Begin with a positive greeting, state today's date, provide current openings for appointments, and ask for the sale.

Here's a sample of an outgoing voice mail message:

"Hello. You have reached [your name] with [your company's name]. We are dedicated to serving you and scheduling your appointment. Today is [Day, Month, Date, Year], and we're booking inspections for the remainder of the week.

"We're currently busy helping another client. We're sorry to miss your call, but both morning and afternoon appointments are available.

"To schedule an inspection, please leave a message about your property, including square footage and age, and your preferred day for the inspection, including whether you need a morning or afternoon appointment.

"All calls will be returned, and we'll call to confirm your appointment as soon as we're available.

"We appreciate your business. Thanks again for calling, and have a great day!"

The Appointment Isn't Automatic

So the question becomes, "How do I maximize the number of inspections that result from incoming calls if many of the people who call me are just shopping?" The answer is to make the processes presented in this section of the book a part of your everyday operations and to make the phone presentation and closing techniques a part of every business call you take. Doing this will maximize each call and increase your inspection volume because you've made a lasting impression through your unmatched professionalism. During the first six months you're in business, the snowball effect will occurs, and as you do more marketing and stay in sight, your business will grow.

Some inspectors think that the agents and buyers should call them just because the inspectors are technically adept and can find all the defects in the house. While this may be true to a point, even the best of products and services *don't sell themselves*. If they did, we wouldn't have so many TV commercials to watch, ads to read on the Internet and in newspapers and magazines, and billboards to look at while we drive along the freeway.

Agents and buyers must *know* you're in business, *feel* good about you as a person, and understand the *value* you bring to your work that separates you from the competition (that is, the agent's favorite inspector). In other words, booking the inspection is not automatic just because the phone rings.

To reduce liability, agents may give out the names of three inspectors to their buyers. Although many buyers go with their agent's first choice, more often than not, they will call all three companies. The difference in your inspection volume is determined by how well you handle the calls. When clients call, they're shopping. Some are shopping price; others, quality. Some customers may not know exactly what they're shopping for, but they may want to choose a home inspector themselves, rather than trust their agent completely.

Clearly, the focus of your phone presentation needs to be on quality and value. The agent has already pointed out the features and benefits of a home inspection, so from the first phone call, your job is to set yourself apart from the competition through quality and professionalism. Your goal is to build value in your services so that a $20 or $50 price difference is less likely to be an issue.

You show quality through professionalism by using excellent communications skills, being prepared, building good rapport, and providing excellent service. This translates into professionalism that separates you from the competition. You build value by taking extra time to educate the caller on your services and the scope of your inspection and asking if he or she has any concerns about the property. Each of these areas is covered in the pages that follow. Read and reread them until you have a full understanding of how to accomplish these goals during every call. It will make the difference in how many inspections you book.

When the time comes to hire an assistant to take your calls, use this manual as a training guide to prepare your new employee in how to handle every function you delegate the same way you have done since the company began doing business.

Excellent Communication Skills Illustrate Quality

The communication skills you learn in class and this manual serve the same purpose for the call as they do in marketing and on an inspection. A good inspection company *educates* the caller about the inspection process; uses *people skills* to put the customer at ease and build *rapport*; and establishes a *positive relationship* with every caller regardless of whether they book the inspection now, later, or never.

Building Rapport

As a home inspector, you're detail-oriented and provide a technical service for a living. This doesn't mean you can afford to be impersonal or, even worse, cold over the phone. Ask the buyers questions about the property and get them talking about why they chose their home. Ask if they have any concerns about the condition of the property and describe what you will do to uncover any defects in these areas. This puts the buyers at ease about choosing you as their inspector and builds value in the fee you charge. Once you have covered these items and pointed out that some items cannot be inspected (for example, obstructed areas and wall cavities), tell the buyers the price and give them a couple of options for dates and times.

Your goal of building rapport and value in your services should include educating every caller about the inspection process, making the appointment fit his or her busy schedule, and building trust by taking responsibility for the caller's understanding of the report findings.

Educating the Caller Builds Value

Many buyers may not have had an inspection in the last five to seven years. The industry has matured and advanced by leaps and bounds in that time—especially if a licensing law has been passed in your state since a buyer's last purchase. In fact, it's likely that a buyer's last inspection, if there was one at all, wasn't performed up to the standards you learned in class. Feedback that many inspectors get from sellers is, "I wish you had done the inspection when I bought this place. The guy we had wasn't nearly as thorough."

This is why it's so important to educate the buyer over the phone about what you will and won't do. Your competition may not take the time to describe the basics over the phone and, as a result, will make you appear more professional and thorough and thus the better candidate for the job. Before giving the caller the price, describe how you begin with the outside of the house and work your way to the interior, touching briefly on each area covered by the SOPs.

More details on the phone presentation will be provided later in this section and will give you specific wording to use.

The Call

Let's look at the information you're most likely to need when scheduling an inspection:

- Buyer's name

- Type of inspection

- Property data

    —Address/Major cross streets

    —Square footage

    —Age

- Inspections and add-ons

    —Radon

—Pools

—Spas

—Wood-destroying insects (WDIs) and wood-destroying organisms (WDOs)

With this information, you're ready to educate the caller about your services and the scope of the inspection. Then you can give the caller the price and ask for the inspection *without pausing*. After the inspection is scheduled, you should discuss a few key points with the client before you end the conversation.

- Inform the client of the length of time you expect to spend on the inspection.

- Encourage the client to attend the inspection.

- Ask about the client's specific concerns about the property. Has the client noticed potential problems?

- Remind the client that all utilities must be turned on for you to perform a proper inspection.

- Request that all areas of the property be accessible, including the following:

  —Attic

  —Basement/crawl space

  —Electrical panel

  —Water heater

  —Locked or gated areas (Ensure that someone, usually the Realtor, will have necessary keys or entry codes.)

- Request that any pets be confined or removed from the property during the inspection.

- Ask the client if he or she has any questions about the process.

- Thank the client for his or her business.

- Confirm the date and time once again.

If all of this sounds complicated and too much to remember, a sample presentation will get you started. As stated earlier, it is important for you to internalize the presentation and make it your own so that you sound natural and confident. You can't expect clients or their agent to be confident in you unless you sound confident yourself.

Incoming Call Presentation

Thank you for calling [your company's name]. This is [your name]. How may I help you?

Client: I'm calling about your prices for a home inspection.

Sure, I can help you with that. The pricing depends on the property we're looking at. If I can ask you a few questions about the property, I'll let you know exactly what the inspection will cost.

You're buying the home? Okay. May I have your name, please? I'm going to write that down so that I can keep the quote on file for you.

(Optional) In what general area (city, suburb, side of town) is the home located? I don't need the exact address right now.

Is this a single-family home? What style is it? About how many square feet would you say it is [First name]? Do you know how old the home is? Okay. And how many bedrooms does it have? How many bathrooms? Does the home have any fireplaces or wood-burning stoves? How many?

Does the home have a basement or a crawl space? (Basement Is that a full basement? (Crawl space) Is that a dirt crawl space? And do you know if it has a dirt cover?

[First name], do you know how many furnaces/heat pumps/boilers the home has? Does it have central air-conditioning? How many water heaters? Does the property have more than one electrical service?

We're almost finished. I just need to ask about the garage. Is it an attached garage? Okay. Is that a two-car garage?

Can you give me an idea of what the sales price of the home is? Thank you. Have we covered all of the features of the house? Is there anything you think I've missed? Okay. That's it then.

The price of the home inspection for this property will be [dollar amount]. *(Do not pause.)* This inspection will take two to three hours to complete. It may take longer than that, [first name], which you may find helpful to know because we recommend that you be there to make sure you're comfortable with the inspection.

We invite you to accompany the inspector and watch throughout the inspection. This is your service. [Your company's name] is working for you, and it's a good educational tour of the home. The inspector will tell you what's happening while he (or she) is inspecting the home and let you know what he (or she) is finding. Of course, the inspector will answer any questions you have during the inspection.

The inspector will write the report as he (or she) inspects the home. That's a 30-page bound (or computerized) report. After the inspection, the inspector will sit down with you and review each page of the report. You'll get your copy to take home with you; you won't have to wait for it.

We recommend you take the report home and read it from cover to cover so that you fully understand the inspection findings. It's a good idea to do that before you release the contingency of having the home inspected. You can also call the inspector to clear up any questions you might have before closing the deal.

Do you have any questions you'd like to ask about the inspection? I'd be happy to answer them.

(If asked questions you can't answer) I'm sorry, [first name], I don't know the answer to that. I can have an inspector call you back, or I can call you back as soon as I have an answer.

(Optional) If you like I can tell you a little more about the inspection. Okay. Now stop me if I'm giving you too much information. Just interrupt me anytime you want.

The inspector will start outside by looking at the exterior—the windows, caulking, siding, and foundation. He (or she) will look at the landscaping to see if any areas are causing drainage problems. The inspector will check the roof by looking at the roof coverings, chimneys, flashings, gutters, and downspouts.

The inspector will take another look at the roof from the inside, from the attic, where he (or she) will look at the roof board, rafters, or trusses. He (or she) will even check the insulation for you.

The inspector will go through the inside, checking the condition of the ceilings, floors, and walls, checking the operation of the doors and windows. He (or she) will do a random testing of the electrical outlets – checking all outlets near water for possible safety hazards. The inspector also will be checking for water problems such as leaking around showers and tubs. He (or she) will check to see that you have adequate water pressure.

In the addition, the inspector will remove the front panel from the electrical box, making sure everything is wired properly and letting you know what kind of electrical service you have.

The inspector also has testing equipment used to check the furnace for a carbon monoxide or gas leak.

(Where applicable) In the basement, the foundation walls will be inspected to see if they're plumb and to determine whether any structural weakness may need to be monitored or whether a specialist should be called in. The plumbing also will be inspected from the basement for leaking and corroded pipes.

Well, that's a brief description of what will happen, [first name]. Do you have any more questions for me?

[First name], did you have a particular day in mind for the inspection? Okay. I can schedule you for [time] or [time]. Which one would be better for you?

Okay. I'll put you on the schedule for [time] and [date]. What's the address of the property we'll be inspecting for you? And your present address? I'll need your mobile number in case I need to call you before the inspection. Thank you. Can you give me the name of the real estate agent you're working with? That's the agent who's representing you, right? Do you have his (or her) phone number? Great. What real estate company is he (or she) with? Okay, can you tell me how you heard about our company?

(Optional) I should mention, [first name], that we also do radon inspections. Do you want to know about that service?

(Your company's name) follows the EPA standards for radon inspections. And the EPA recommends we place two detectors at the site. We use charcoal canisters or continuous radon monitors, which is the most accurate short-term test available and is recognized by all relocation companies. By short-term, I mean that we have to leave the detectors in the house for only 48 hours to get accurate results. After the detectors are picked up, they're sent to our lab and you'll have the results within 10 to 14 days. We'll tell you the level of radon in the home and explain what that means. I can have the inspector perform the test if you wish. The cost would only be [dollar amount].

Now, before I let you go, let me confirm the price I gave you. That's [dollar amount] for the home inspection. That fee will be collected at the inspection site. Mention the type of payments you accept.

We'll see you on (day) at (time). You should call your Realtor and confirm that the appointment works for him (or her) and the seller. If you need to change the appointment, give us a call. If I don't hear from you, I'll assume that everything's all right.

(Not now callers) You're not ready to schedule the appointment yet?

(Talk to spouse) Of course. You'll certainly want to do that, although I could pencil in an appointment to reserve a time for you. You can always cancel it.

(No offer yet) Oh, I see. Well, I hope you'll call us back after you make the offer to purchase. And good luck with the house.

(Still shopping) That's all right. I know you're looking for the best home inspection service. Just make sure you ask each company whether it's certified and whether it carries professional liability insurance (that's like malpractice insurance a doctor has to have).

I'll share with you what separates us from other home inspection companies so that you'll remember us. First, you should know that our highly skilled inspectors are certified by the American Home Inspectors Training Institute. AHIT has been training home inspectors for over two decades. AHIT teaches all of its inspectors to exceed nationally recognized standards, even those required by [your state]. We're serious about having the best inspectors.

Another thing that sets us apart is that we're fully insured. We have errors and omissions insurance as well as liability. That's important for you to know in case anything goes wrong.

The best in inspector training and full insurance coverage are two areas in which some companies cut corners because of the expense. But remember that [your company's name] has both. And don't forget about the free video and manual we have for you.

I'll keep your price quote on hand, [first name], so that when you call back, we can set up an appointment right away. And listen, please call me back if you have any questions or I can help you in any way.

The presentation should take about five to seven minutes from start to finish without interruptions. Taking less time may mean that you're going through the motions of an order taker and not building enough value for the customer to justify hiring you just to save a few dollars. Taking too long is overkill and may result in losing a customer, or even worse, sending the message to the real estate agent that you overelaborate on your report findings the same way you do on the phone. This could result in missed opportunities.

Practice and rehearse this presentation before you are ready to take calls. Doing so will make you sound fluid, confident, and professional. These are the qualities that will set you apart from the competition and get you more appointments.

OFFICE PLAN

The behind-the-scenes part of a business contributes a great deal to its success. *AHIT* knows that the smooth operation of your home inspection will allow you to concentrate on providing quality home inspections and marketing your services to the real estate community.

Running your business will require a range of skills and a personal commitment to having an office that operates smoothly—even if you don't enjoy the dedication it requires. You'll be well rewarded for it.

This manual provides a system of office operations and procedures. These pages describe how to get your business started, what needs to be done on an ongoing basis, and how to manage your employees—everything you need to know.

THE BUSINESS

You will have chosen the date on which your home inspection business will begin operations. This section details those business tasks that need to be completed before that day arrives.

Legal Matters

One of the first steps you must take to get ready for business is to see your attorney. You should do the following:

- **Establish a legal business entity.** Discuss with your attorney which type of business organization is appropriate for you.

    ◦ Corporation

    ◦ LLC

    ◦ Sole proprietorship

    ◦ Partnership

    ◦ Other

- Get a federal ID number for your business.

- Name your business and register it.

Ensure that you're compliant with the law. At the same time your attorney is handling all the necessary paperwork that goes along with creating the legal business entity, ask that you be fully informed about what steps you must follow to be in full compliance with the law. Your attorney should be able to inform you or direct you to information about compliance with the following:

—Laws, rules, and regulations of governmental authorities and agencies

—Wage, hour, and other laws and regulations of the federal, state, and local governments

—Preparation and filing of tax returns

—Any city and state permits, certificates, registrations, and licenses that you need to conduct your business

Insurance

All necessary insurance policies must be in place by the time you open your business. You should discuss with your attorney, accountant, insurance agent, and advisers, what coverage's are right for you and your business.

The following policies are recommended:

• Professional liability insurance (also referred to as errors and omissions insurance): Covers you in case you make a mistake on an inspection

• General liability insurance: Covers you in case you damage someone's property; covers your offices and other general needs

• Employer's liability insurance: Covers you and your employees for work-related bodily injury and disease and provides worker's compensation insurance as described by law

• Vehicle insurance: Covers employees who drive as part of their employment

Banking, Accounting, and Taxes

One of your first steps after creating your business will be to set up a checking account in your business's name, using a local bank. You should need only one business account. When shopping for the right bank, you might ask if the bank will provide a payroll service at no cost or at a nominal fee. (This can save you an enormous amount of time and money if you have employees and need to hire a payroll firm to do the job.) If not, numerous payroll services are available or your accountant may be able to handle this for you. You probably won't need this service for a while, but it is wise to plan for future growth.

When you choose the checks for your account, you might consider using carbon copy checks, providing you with a copy of each check that you write. You'll need to keep excellent records of every transaction, so if you tend to be sloppy about writing information on check stubs, carbon copy checks may solve your problem. Also look for a bank that has a solid online banking solution. This can save you a great deal of time and even the need to write checks manually.

Now that you are running a business, you'll have to keep accurate accounting records. Quicken software allows you to enter incoming and outgoing amounts to a check register and to reconcile monthly activity to your bank statement. You may want to check it out to see if it fits with your business. Quicken also prints out the basic accounting and tax preparation reports you'll need to turn over to an accountant.

You must make a decision about how the accounting for your business is going to be done. You have options. What you decide to do depends on how you would rate yourself in relation to the accounting process. This ranges from "I don't know anything about accounting" all the way to "I'm a CPA." It also depends on whether you have employees and need payroll capabilities. *AHIT* has this suggestion about how to manage your accounting needs:

- Basic accounting. For the most part, you will have to do this on your own. Basic accounting requires that you enter all customer records, record incoming and outgoing amounts, reconcile activity to your bank statement each month, and report activity in the form of profit and loss statements.

- Annual accounting. For this, you must hire an accountant to prepare your year-end reconciliation, profit and loss statements, and balance sheet. You should locate an accounting firm up front and let it review the basic accounting procedures you're going to follow. Any procedures can be adjusted then so that your records will be in the format the accountant needs at the end of your first year.

  —Payroll. It's not wise for you to do your own payroll. There are so many considerations—withholding FICA, FUTA, wage and tax reporting, insurance contributions and more. In fact, Quicken software does not have this capability. However, many services such as ADP and Zenefits will provide this service at a reasonable cost.

- Taxes. You should definitely have your accountant prepare your annual tax returns. He or she should prepare your quarterly taxes as well. Even if Quicken allows you to prepare your own taxes, it's a good idea to hire an accountant to handle all tax reporting. Note that you can tag each item in the chart of accounts for tax purposes, which will help your accountant prepare your final tax reports.

Services Offered

You'll have to decide the scope of services you're going to offer in your business.

Your company may choose to offer one or more of the optional products/services, including:

1. Buyer Inspection

2. Seller inspection

   a. Review with buyer inspection

3. Radon testing

4. Home maintenance inspection

    a. Home Maintenance Inspection Plan

5. Commercial inspections

6. Mold testing

7. Energy audits

8. In-progress construction inspection

9. Condo association inspection

10. Roof certification inspection

11. Pest inspection

12. Permit research

13. Expert testimony

You'll find descriptions of each of these services in Chapter 1.

    Other **optional services** are available that you may want to offer your customers:

- DILHR weatherization inspections

- Swimming pool inspections

- Well and septic inspections

- Lead inspections

- Asbestos inspections

You should get information about your state's training and/or certification requirements for performing the various types of inspections and testing. Some states may require you to obtain certifications or licensing for some or all of the services.

Pricing Structure

Word gets around real estate circles, and agents know whose prices are too high and may be suspicious of services that are offered at prices that seem too low. Because the home inspection business is a referral business, what the agent thinks about your pricing structure is very important.

    It's almost impossible to have a flat rate for all home inspections. Firms that try it typically end up charging too much for typical homes and too little for larger homes. The amount of time you spend inspecting a home depends on the home's features, which is why *AHIT* developed a pricing structure that prices each home on its own merits.

BASE RATE for typical home
+   ADD-ONS for extra features
TOTAL PRICE for the home inspection

AHIT's pricing structure is what can be called a base plus add-ons. Here's how it works. For each territory, a base price is established for a typical single-family house, which is about 2000 square feet, has two bathrooms, and has a single HVAC system.

Any deviation from the features of a typical home, or additional features, are priced and added to the base price. These additional features include the following:

- Each bathroom over the typical two

- Each additional HVAC system

- A dirt crawl space

- A three-car or larger garage

- An apartment over a garage

- An outbuilding such as a barn or an extra garage

- Electricity, heat, and water in an outbuilding

- Square footage over 2000 (possibly increments of 500 square feet)

- Age, especially if older than 100 years

You will have to determine how much you can charge for any of the add-ons noted above. You may decide to add $25 to $50 for each item. Think about how much time it takes to inspect those add-on features and work to get paid for that extra time. For example, if it takes 15 to 20 minutes to inspect an HVAC system completely and your time is valued at $200 per hour, then 15 minutes is worth $50.

So if your base fee is, for example, $300, your incremental increase is $50 per 500 square feet, and the call comes in for a 4200-square-foot home with three HVAC systems for which you charge $50 each, your pricing would look like this:

Base Fee: $300
2200-square-foot add-on: $250
Two extra HVAC systems: $100
Total: $650

NOTE: The pricing guide above is just an example and is not meant to provide pricing for your services. You must determine your company's pricing structure.

For two-family dwellings, the base price is the single-family base plus an additional amount. For three or more units, you establish a base price. In each case, you apply add-ons for extra features. The base multiple-family dwellings are defined as follows:

- A two-family home with one bathroom each and two furnaces, with different base prices for the following:

    —Up-and-down

    —Side-by-side

- For three or more units, one bathroom and one furnace each.

A WORD OF CAUTION: The pricing structure is *not* to be discussed with the customer. An inspector doesn't say, "Oh, you have another furnace. That will be $50 more." You total the prices silently while gathering information about the house and quote one final price to the customer.

Before you determine prices for your business, do some pricing research on those home inspection firms you consider to be your chief competitors. This research will help you establish a complete pricing structure. If all the homes in your area have a dirt crawl space, you may not be able to charge extra for it. This is where your research on the competition comes in handy. Knowing the typical pricing structure of the other inspectors near you will keep you in line so that your pricing is not too high or low. *Never sell based on being the lowest price.*

1. Ask agents. Probably the best pricing research you can do is to talk with agents. Just ask what a typical home inspection costs. And ask how much the inspection would be if the house was much larger than normal or was quite expensive.

2. Call your competitors. Begin by calling your competitors and asking for the price of an inspection on a typical home, as described above. It's important to keep the details the same with each call so that you can compare apples to apples when you're done. Next, call each competitor again, this time adding extra features to the house. Give it more bathrooms, an extra furnace, etc. Repeat the process with a two- or three-family home.

3. Determine your own prices. There's nothing exact about using this research. Even so, you should be getting a general idea of an average price for inspections in your area for a typical home and for more complex homes.

Choose a base price and experiment with various add-on prices. Compare total prices with those of your competitors. You need to be especially careful with add-ons. Your base price may be competitive, but with the add-ons, you may find yourself on the high end of the market, where you don't want to be.

For some home inspection businesses, there may be distinct difference between areas as to what the medium-range price is. What is the middle of the market in one suburb may be on the high end in another. In that case, you should establish a base price for each area.

Phone Answering

Almost all of your business will come to you over the phone. Your referral base of agents usually suggests that their clients call three or four different home inspection services to find the one that's right for them. So when a call comes in, it means that someone is shopping for a home inspector—shopping, not buying.

Getting the appointment from a shopper is not automatic. Prospective customers may think that they're shopping just for price, but, in fact, they're looking for much more. They're also assessing how professional your company is and whether it can do a good job for them. You've got to be able to provide what they need and close the sale.

A variety of daytime phone-answering options are discussed here—some acceptable and some not. The unacceptable options are discussed only to show you why they don't work.

- **Answering machines don't work during business hours.** People will hang up and pass you by. You see, they're shopping, and if you're not there, they'll call the next inspector on the list. That means you lose a sale. *An answering machine is not an option for daytime calls.*

- **Voice mail doesn't work during business hours either.** The response is the same as above. People are looking for someone to talk to, and the sale is lost. This is not an option during working hours.

- **Professionally answering your phone works.** Having a trained professional scheduler to book your inspections will increase business faster than almost anything else. If you cannot afford to hire a full-time staff member, professional answering services, such as America's Call Center, are available that specialize in running call centers for inspectors. You will have much less control, but it's a better option than the first two.

- **Phone answered by a family member when your office is in your home can be counterproductive.** Too many independent home inspectors lose business when the phone is answered casually, when the phone is answered by the wrong person, or when screaming children are heard in the background. This is an option *only if*:

  —A family member has been trained about home inspection and in closing sales.

  —The family member is present during all working hours and is free to pick up the phone immediately.

  —The phone is not used for other purposes.

  —No untrained family members answer the phone.

  —There is no background "family" noise.

Your solution to the phone-answering situation is one of the most important decisions you'll make in setting up your business. Because a large portion of your business will come over the phone, you need to be confident that whoever answers can capture the sale.

NOTE: If you have your own scheduler during working hours, the phones should be covered in the evenings and on weekends. Voice mail may be used during off-hours.

THE OFFICE

This section presents those office tasks that need to be completed before your first day of business. It includes suggestions for finding office space andgetting office equipment.

The Right Space

Home inspection businesses that want to have their business in their home should consider the following:

- Dedicating a separate room or rooms to office use

- Keeping the room, computer system, other equipment, and phones secure from children.

- Having the required business phone lines in addition to a home phone

Your office needs will depend on the size of the home inspection operation. If you're starting out with just yourself as the office manager and sole inspector, a 1-room office is all you'll need. Even if you hire a scheduler to cover the phone, a 1-room office should be adequate, since you'll be out of the office during working hours doing inspections. More space can be acquired as additional inspectors are hired.

For home inspectors starting out with a scheduler and several inspectors, the office will require more space at the beginning. The larger volume business may have a general manager in the office during working hours and may require a second scheduler. Certainly, more files and storage space will be required. And increased inspector traffic makes the office a busier place. We suggest at least a 2-room office or larger, depending on the number of employees.

SPACE REQUIREMENTS

One-person office: one room, 150 to 200 square feet

Inspector and scheduler: one room, 150 to 200 square feet

Multi-employee business: two rooms, 300 to 400 square feet

More space is required for a very large operation.

Having 150 to 200 square feet for the single office takes into account the room needed for a computer, fax, and phone setup; for the workspace; and for files and storage.

Recommended Equipment

Some equipment can be leased or purchased depending on how you want to handle it.

Personal computer—Look into a two-in-one laptop that you can use in the field for taking notes.

- Computer software

  —The latest Windows operating system or iOS for Apple computers

  —Quicken (or another relevant accounting software)

  —Word (or other word-processing software)

- Computer printer: Any modern laser printer with scanning and faxing capabilities should be sufficient. At a small volume, this should meet all of your copying needs. That being said, as your business grows you may want to consider getting a stand-alone copy machine.

If you have your own scheduler, you'll need two lines:

- One business line for all incoming business calls and voice mail for after-hour calls. This is the number on your website, your business cards, and other promotional materials.

- One dedicated line for the fax machine. (If your printer has a scanner, you can eliminate the fax machine by using Web-based faxing services.)

Additional Equipment and Supplies

This section of the manual lists office furniture and general office supplies recommended by *AHIT* for each home inspection office.

You don't need to invest a great deal of money in new office furniture. The list provided here is for functional needs. One concern is that you have enough working space as well as surface space for equipment and that you have plenty of space to track the flow of paperwork your business will produce. Another concern is that you have enough storage for all of the supplies that will be needed. It's recommended that each office have the following furnishings:

- An 8-foot table used to hold office equipment (fax machine, computer, printer, and copy machine).

- A surface to be used as working space. This could be a desk or a 5-foot table.

- Two or more chairs, depending on how the office is set up.

- A 5-foot activity table used to manage the flow of inspection paperwork and inspection supplies. Don't overlook this surface space.

- A four-drawer file cabinet to be used for customer files and business files.

- A bookcase used to store operational manuals, software manuals, reference books, and some supplies.

  One or more storage cabinets to store office, marketing, and inspection supplies.

- A large area wall map used to locate streets and roads in your territory. (Your inspection area should be visible at a glance.) This does not replace using Google Maps, Google Earth, or MapQuest, for example, but it is helpful in seeing distances between inspections.

- A bulletin board used to post schedules and reminders.

- A slotted file holder for storing forms that are used regularly. This could be a horizontal one for your desk or a small shelved one to hang on the wall.

The following general office supplies are necessities:

- Printer paper and toner or cartridge

- File pockets and some folders

- Pens, blue or black, for writing inspection reports

- Stapler and staples

- Paper clips

- Pushpins

And you'll probably need a number of miscellaneous office supplies as well, such as:

- Calculator

- Pencils and pencil sharpener

Notepads

- Legal pads

- Rubber bands

- Tape

- 9 × 12 mailers

- Labels

ONGOING OFFICE PROCEDURES

Complaint Handling

One of the most important ongoing activities you'll oversee is handling of complaints. Complaints should be given top priority and handled immediately.

Liability ranks as one of the top issues in the home inspection profession. Inspectors need to face the fact that no matter how "perfectly" they and their inspectors perform home inspections, complaints and threats of lawsuits will come up. We live in a litigious society, and consumers are quick to act on both the reality and *perception* of accountability by a home inspection business for problems with their homes.

Inspectors will experience complaint calls, both reasonable and unreasonable, and will become involved in handling those complaints. A plan of action includes the following:

- Correct insurance coverage

- Proactive approach of aggressive prevention

- Inspector participation in complaint handling

- Immediate complaint handling

Proactive Prevention

The steps that inspectors must take to manage complaints and lawsuits are presented here briefly, but in more detail in *The Inspection Plan*.

Inspectors should do the following:

- Review the Preinspection Agreement with the customer, making sure the customer understands the following:

  —The definition of an inspection and its content and scope, especially what the inspection does and does not cover.

  —Latent or concealed defects are excluded.

  —The inspector won't be valuing the property or reporting on compliance with codes or regulations.

  —The inspector isn't an insurer or a guarantor against defects.

- Perform a quality inspection, paying careful attention to the Don't-Ever-Miss lists or Needing Repair items presented in the *Property Inspection Report*.

- **Ask the customer to be present during the inspection,** communicating constantly what you are doing and what you have discovered, as well as the importance of each issue. You never want to hear a client say, "The inspector didn't tell me it was that important" or "If the inspector would have emphasized its importance, I would have asked the seller to repair it."

- **Show customers your dedication** to the job by working hard, intently, and professionally.

- **Write a clear, precise report and review its contents** with the customer, pointing out where you've written items of particular importance.

- **Encourage customers to read** the entire *Property Inspection Report* after the inspector leaves.

Complaints Overview

Complaints generally follow a certain pattern. Usually, the customer calls first to state the nature of the complaint. You (or the inspector) may be able to settle the complaint without help from an attorney or the insurance company by paying for repairs, paying out a settlement amount, or getting the customer to drop the claim. But depending on the severity of the problem, the situation may not be settled quickly or you may have trouble bringing the issue to a close. Then you can expect to get a call from the customer's attorney, followed by a letter from the attorney. The next step may be receiving a summons from the customer's attorney.

Complaints *generally* follow this pattern, but you could be surprised by a summons in the mail, having received no prior warning. In any case, when the summons arrives, it's time to bring in the professionals.

When you first experience complaint calls or receive a summons, it can be a scary experience. You'll find them less distressing after you've been through a few.

When a Complaint Arrives

Even when inspectors follow the guidelines listed earlier, complaint calls will come in. Sometimes, an inspector made a mistake, and sometimes, the caller has no basis for a legitimate claim. However, each incoming call should be handled the same way, following these basic procedures:

- Use a Complaint Information Form to gather the necessary information.

- Remind customers of the 72-hour rule in the Pre-Inspection Agreement, which states that the customer must notify you 72 hours prior to repairing or replacing any system or component about which they're complaining. So, assuming that the customer hasn't already hired someone to make repairs or purchased any replacements before calling you, request that he or she honor the 72-hour period so that you can come over to see what the problem is.

- Tell customers that the inspector (owner, general manager) will call them back. Do *not* try to deal with the complaint during the incoming call. Promising that you'll deal with the problem right away and call back gives the customer time to cool off and realize that you're taking the complaint seriously.

When dealing with complaint calls, remember to take *all* of them seriously and to treat the customers with respect.

Handling the Complaint

The first rule of handling complaints is to address *all* of them immediately, beginning the same day the complaint comes in. Begin by finding the *Property Inspection Report* in the customer file. In a multi-inspector home inspection business, turn the complaint over to the inspector to handle. Work with the inspector. If it is your business, you should deal with the complaint after speaking with the inspector and reviewing the report.

Complaints are handled differently depending on what type of problem it is and whether the inspector is responsible for the problem. Complaints can be divided into the following general categories:

1. Damage caused by something the inspector did or didn't do. Here are some examples:

- The inspector turned the furnace off and didn't turn it back on in the winter, causing plumbing pipes to freeze and burst.

- The inspector filled up a bathtub and left the bathroom to inspect another room and the tub overflowed causing damage to the flooring.

- The inspector unplugged the refrigerator, resulting in spoiled food.

You (or the inspector) should call the customer immediately and go see the problem for yourself. If the damage is less than the liability deductible, you may decide to take care of the problem yourself rather than turn it over to your insurance company. Schedule whatever needs to be done as soon as you can. Hire someone to fix what needs fixing, pay for repairs, fix it yourself, replace spoiled food, etc.

2. Something was missed during the inspection. This is when you or your inspectors are at fault for missing something. There is so much potential of this happening, which is why the Don't-Ever-Miss lists in *The Property Inspection Report* are important. Here are a few examples:

- The inspector didn't note a cracked or broken structural component.

- The inspector missed faulty wiring.

- The inspector didn't note the lack of a heat run into a specific room.

You (or the inspector) should call the customer immediately and go see the problem. Schedule whatever needs to be done as soon as you can. Hire someone to repair structures and wiring, put in heat runs, etc.

    For big-ticket items such as replacing furnaces, turn the claims over to your insurance company for settlement.

3. A problem was noted in the *Property Inspection Report*, but the customer didn't follow your recommendations. There are many examples of this as well. Here are some:

- The inspector noted that the furnace showed signs of rusting and suggested that a furnace expert be called in to check it. The owner didn't call in an expert and now has furnace problems. The customer claims that it's your fault.

- The inspector noted that a structural engineer should be called in to check the crack in the basement wall. The owner didn't call in an engineer and now has more serious problems with the wall, claiming that it's your fault.

These problems aren't your fault, and a review of the inspection report proves it. The reason inspectors review the report with customers after inspections and encourage them to read the report is to avoid these calls. It doesn't always work. Many customers call anyway.

The first thing you should do is call the real estate agent to find out if the agent is named in the case and what his or her position is. It pays to know this before getting back to the customer. Sometimes, if you settle the case, you save the agent and create goodwill with him or her. Then you should immediately call the customer and point out what the report says—that the problem had been noted—and that your company is not responsible for the problem. Explain the situation in the return phone call and that you have it documented in your inspection report.

Because these problems are often expensive to fix, customers may not back down. During your phone conversation, suggest that they find the report so that you can review the specific page with them now. Maintaining your respect for the customer, do what you can to get the customer to admit his or her error and drop the claim.

These situations sometimes call for special consideration depending on how upset the customer is. You should measure winning in this situation against the goodwill that might result if you make a settlement offer. You may be smoothing out a tough situation for the agent. So even if you're right, doing something for the customer can help ensure a future referral.

One suggestion for a token payment is to return the inspection fee. Anytime you return money or pay for repairs, you must get the client to sign a release form for further and future liability. Ask your attorney for a release form to use for this purpose.

The results of helping people with problems might be greater than you can imagine. In each scenario, try to determine whether paying a claim will bring in more referrals. This can help ease your mind about any payouts you make. Of course, if the customer refuses a small settlement and pursues the claim, you should turn the case over to your attorney or insurance company.

4. **Nuisance calls.** There's no other way to describe them. These calls can come in months or years after an inspection and can be about any number of problems not caused by or missed by your inspectors. Some examples:

   • A faucet that started to leak several months after the inspection

   • A carpet that has begun to smell of pets now that damp weather has set in

   • Wallpaper that started to peel several months after the inspection

Call this customer back immediately and explain why such problems are not your responsibility. The company has not warranted the *ongoing condition* of systems and components in the house. The condition *at the time of inspection* was reported, and that condition can change. Try to explain the situation, being firm that this isn't your responsibility.

In some of these cases, you may think that the situation is over only to have the customer call back and start all over again with his or her complaint. If the customer won't back off or you judge that settlement is needed for goodwill, you may want to offer $50 just to get rid of the situation.

The Release Form

When you settle with a customer on a complaint, send a letter asking him or her to sign a release form. This form, in exchange for a named sum of money, discharges your home inspection business from all liability and from all present and future claims. In the letter, the customer is asked to return to your office the signed form and the *Property Inspection Report* from the original inspection before you send him or her the settlement check. File all papers concerning incoming complaints and settlements, including the release form, in the customer's file.

OPERATIONAL BUSINESS ACTIVITIES

DAILY ACTIVITIES

You should follow the daily procedures provided in this section religiously. Focusing on these details will make your business run smoothly. This section of the manual includes many details about how to do every daily task. Actually, it's meant to serve as instructional material for whoever in your office is assigned these tasks. Use this section initially to learn how to do the job and then to check on details as you need them.

Here's an overview of the daily office activities of a home inspection business:

- Taking incoming appointment calls.

- Tracking inspections by:

  —Filling in an appointment sheet for each new appointment.

  —Entering all appointments in the Customer database.

  —Copying appointment sheets.

  —Keeping a software or Web-based appointment program up to date.

- Preparing for inspections by:

  — Organizing active appointments.

  — Printing out a schedule of appointments.

  — Having supplies ready.

- Following up on inspections by:

  — Filling in the post-inspection forms.

  — Handling radon tests and results.

  — Doing the follow-up work.

  — Taking care of new Plan members (if you offer this optional product).

- Handling the business end of the job:

  —Matching checks to each job.

  —Preparing checks for deposit.

  —Preparing billing invoices when necessary. (Ideally, payment should be collected before or at the time of each inspection.)

  —Entering payments into the customer database.

- Protecting your business by:

  —Backing up computer data.

A Cash Business

The home inspection business is a cash business, meaning that fees are collected at the time of the job. Except for rare circumstances, customers are not invoiced for later payment.

When appointments are made, customers should be told that they are expected to pay for the inspection at the inspection site. Inspectors should be trained to get the payment after they complete the inspection. They shouldn't let customers off the hook. If a customer has forgotten his or her checkbook, inspectors can be resourceful in collecting the fee. Some inspectors have even gone with customers to an automatic teller machine while they withdraw cash. You should keep your business a cash business and not invoice customers any more than is absolutely necessary.

The Customer Database

Systems such as www.inspectionsupport.net (ISN) and other tracking software programs can be an inspector's best business tool. Diligently entering information into the customer database gives you access to the important information you'll need to run the business. When you put the information in, this is what you get out:

- Overall appointment schedule

- Working schedule the scheduler will use

- Cash receipts from jobs done

- Revenue from jobs done

- Report stating royalties due

- Payroll documentation for each inspector

- Invoices for outstanding fees due

- List of outstanding fees due

- Activity report of types of inspections done

- Statistics from opinion forms for inspector quality control

- Marketing reports and promotional letters

The Appointment Sheet/Log

Almost all of your business activity is recorded and tracked by the information on the appointment sheet or log. And that makes this sheet/log the single most important item in keeping your business running smoothly. This sheet/log must be filled in for every appointment that is made.

If you are using a manual system, your scheduler should have several copies of the appointment sheet available. If you are using a computer system, your scheduler should have this system open and backed up on the computer. The following list tells you what information you need to provide in each section of the appointment sheet/log.

- Record the appointment day, date, and time, which should be written, for example, as Monday 4/8/16 3 p.m. You should write it this way so that you can confirm the day and the date with the customer.

- Record the name of the inspector.

- Record the type of inspection and who ordered the inspection.

- Note the area for a radon pickup day, date, and time. This is filled in after the radon inspection so that it can be recorded on the radon tracking form and inspectors won't miss the pickup.

  If your company offers other services, they also should be noted on the schedule sheet/log. Then inspectors can easily check them off or use them as reminders.

- For a review inspection, get the seller's name. If you're charging a percentage of the seller's original fee as the review inspection fee, you'll need to refer to the seller's customer record before determining this fee.

- Record information about the agent and the broker or real estate company this customer is working with. If you can, also get the name of the referring company.

- Record information about the property on which the inspection fee will be based. Here is an explanation of some of the terms used:

  —Property is a single-family, multiple-family, or condo

  —The style of the property is ranch, colonial, or Victorian

  —Square footage (Sq. Ft.) and age

—Number of bedrooms and bathrooms

—Number of fireplaces (FP) and whether the house has a wood-burning stove (WB)

—Type of basement

—Type of crawl space (cement or dirt) if there is one

—Number of furnaces and presence of central air-conditioning (A/C)

—Number of water heaters (W-H) and electric services

—Type of garage as attached or detached and type of garage as one-car (1-c), two-car (2-car), etc.

—Estimate of how long it will take to perform the inspection

- Record the home inspection price, the price for a radon inspection, and the price of any other service to be performed. Calculate the total price.

- Record the date of the call and who took it at the time the appointment is made. The rest of the information is filled in later.

- Record the date the customer paid and the check number when the check is received.

PROCEDURE: When appointment sheets/logs are filled out, they should be put in the customer database or entered in the computer while an order is being taken, if possible. They can be entered directly to the database or uploaded at the end of each day.

WEEKLY ACTIVITIES

This section discusses activities that must be done weekly.

You should consider a business week as running from Monday to Sunday. Here's an overview of the weekly office activities of a home inspection business:

- Tracking weekly inspection monies by:

—Matching each check to each job.

—Preparing checks for deposit.

—Printing out cash, revenue, and invoice reports.

—Reconciling paperwork to reports.

- Every second week, managing employee wages by:

—Printing out payroll documentation.

—Reviewing the payroll documentation.

- Keeping the files up to date by:

  —Filing customer paperwork in the customer file.

  —Filing the batched weekly accounting backup.

  —Filing business records.

- Managing supplies by:

  —Checking the supply inventory.

  —Ordering needed supplies.

Accounting for the Money

At the end of your business week, ending Sunday, you should have the following items for accounting:

- Copies of appointment sheets

- Copies of invoices

- Checks, unless already deposited

- Copies of Home Preservation Plan agreements

The following steps should be taken at the end of each week:

1. Handle anything that hasn't been done during the day. You may have more checks in the accounting that you haven't deposited yet. Compare check amounts one last time against the paperwork. Mark the paperwork when you remove the checks. Put the checks aside for deposit.

2. Sort the paperwork once more. This time sort the paperwork from accounting as follows:

   Group A: This week's paid jobs. Put together the paperwork for jobs performed and *paid for* this week. Include new Plan memberships paid for this week.

   Group B: This week's unpaid jobs. Put together the paperwork for jobs performed this week that are *not yet paid for.*

   Group C: Previous weeks' paid jobs. Put together the paperwork for jobs performed in previous weeks that *were paid* for this week.

   Group D: Previous weeks' unpaid jobs. This last pile contains the paperwork for jobs performed in previous weeks that *still aren't paid.*

1. Calculate totals for each group of paperwork. Add up the fees from each stack of paperwork you sorted. Then find these totals:

   - Cash receipts: The sum of stacks A and C. This is how much money you took in this week.

   - Gross revenues: The sum of stacks A and B. This is the total value of fees for *this* week, whether or not you received payment.

   - Outstanding fees: The sum of stacks B and D. This is the amount of money you haven't collected yet.

2. Put aside the paid jobs for filing. Staple a copy of the Cash Report to the front of the batch of paperwork for this week's paid jobs (A and C). This batch can be set aside for filing. Keep the unpaid jobs in the accounting tray until payment is received.

You may not want to do your own payroll because of the many complicated considerations—withholding, FICA, FUTA, wage and tax reporting, insurance contributions, etc. Have your bank do the payroll or hire a payroll firm to take care of it. Of course, you'll have to supply the necessary documentation that will be the basis of computing the payroll.

Doing the Filing

At the end of each week, in the customer files, file the material you set aside from your follow-up. You should have the appointment sheets, copies of the *Property Inspection Report*, Review Inspection agreements, Plan agreements, copies of follow-up letters, etc. Label a file folder for each customer (last name, first name) and insert their paperwork. File the folders in alphabetical order in the customer files.

You'll also have materials for the business file. One set is the weekly accounting batch—the weekly Cash Report attached to the copies of the appointment sheets, paid invoices, etc. Label a file folder with the ending date of the week for this set of papers. File this material by date in a special accounting records drawer of your business file.

Checking Supplies

Take an inventory of supplies each week and estimate what you'll need for the next month or so. If you're getting low on anything, reorder now.

MONTHLY ACTIVITIES

The following pages describe activities that must be done on a monthly basis— at the end of each calendar month. Here's an overview of the monthly office activities of a home inspection business:

- Tracking monthly inspection monies

- Reconciling your monthly bank statement by:

  —Checking that you've entered all checks and deposits in the check register.

  —Balancing the account.

- Producing accounting records by:

    —Printing out the Profit and Loss Statement.

    —Printing out the Income and Expense Report.

- Performing ongoing tasks for marketing by:

    —Entering data from opinion form into the customer database.

    —Sending out letters to sell the Plan to customers.

    —Sending anniversary letters to Plan members.

Monthly Accounting Records

The two reports listed below should be printed for your records at the end of each month. They can be printed from Quicken.

- Profit and Loss Statement

- Income and Expense Report

The Profit and Loss Statement shows income and expense totaled by categories, with a profit or loss (income minus expenses) number at the bottom. The Income and Expense Report shows you transactions by category; it provides an itemized list of where your money is being spent each month.

Both of these reports are useful in understanding the overall picture of your finances. They should be filed in your business files. You also may want to talk to your accountant to get suggestions for additional reports that you may need monthly. See the Quicken user's manual for instructions on creating these reports.

Opinion Form Entry

Another task that should be performed each month is to enter into the customer database the information from returned opinion forms. It's okay to let the postcards sit until the end of the month and then enter the data all at once.

There are several uses for statistics from opinion forms:

- Pulling statistics to monitor customers' ratings of your performance.

- Pulling statistics by inspectors' names to monitor how customers rate their performance.

- Pulling statistics by realtors' names to let them know how their clients rate your business.

- Pulling particular statistics to use in promotions.

Monthly Marketing Letters

Three ongoing marketing tasks should be done each month. These tasks refer only to home inspection businesses that offer the optional products in the home preservation product line. You can disregard this section if you don't offer those products.

- Sending out letters to sell the Home Preservation Plan to customers of the buyer and review inspections.

- Sending out letters to Plan members on their anniversary date to encourage them to schedule their checkup inspection.

- Sending out letters to expiring Plan members notifying them of their last chance to schedule an inspection at their fixed Plan price.

You should send these letters on a monthly basis, first sending the letters to sell the Home Preservation Plan to previous customers. Then once some members have signed up for the Plan, you can send letters to them promoting the home preservation inspection. Don't overlook the importance of staying in contact with and in the minds of past and future clients.

YEARLY ACTIVITIES

Activities that need to be done each year are discussed in this section. Tax reporting comes at the end of the calendar year (with quarterly reporting), other activities such as annual accounting need to be done at the end of the company's fiscal year, and still others such as renewing insurance policies come on anniversary dates.

Here's an overview of the yearly activities of a home inspection business.

- Meeting tax requirements by:

    —Delivering needed documents to accountant.

    —Having all tax returns and forms prepared.

    —Filing tax returns.

    —Paying taxes due.

- Completing fiscal year-end accounting by:

    —Delivering needed information to accountant.

    —Having a profit and loss statement and a balance sheet prepared.

- When insurance policies are up for renewal:

    —Reviewing coverage and premiums.

    —Looking for different carriers if necessary.

    —After renewal, sending to headquarters certificates showing compliance with requirements.

- Upon the anniversaries of membership:

  —Renewing association memberships.

  —Renewing Board of REALTORS® affiliation.

  —Paying annual dues.

Taxes

After the end of each calendar year, you will have to deliver the appropriate records to your accountant for the preparation of annual tax returns. You should discuss with your accountant what documents he or she will need. For inspectors with employees, some of these documents will come from the payroll firm that was hired to manage payroll. (Note that you'll be paying taxes on a quarterly basis and will have to work with your accountant each quarter. Only the annual process is described here.)

1. Finish December's monthly close. Make sure you've completed the monthly activities for December—all data entry completed, bank statement reconciled, and accounting reports printed out.

2. Print out documents from your records. You'll have to prepare the following reports for your accountant:

- Yearly Cash Report

- Yearly Profit and Loss Statement. Print out this report from Quicken or another bookkeeping program.

- Yearly Income and Expense Report. Print out this report from Quicken

- Tax Schedule Report. If you've set up Quicken properly with each category in the chart of accounts tagged for its corresponding tax form and line, you'll be able to pull this report. Your accountant may want this report on a computer disk to feed into the accountant's tax preparation software. Quickens user's manual will explain how to transfer this data.

  Gather other necessary records. Ask your accountant what additional information he or she will needs from you. Be prepared to provide other information from your files, such as year-end payroll records, equipment purchases, receipts, and other backup records.

Annual Accounting

1. Complete last month's close. Make sure you've completed the monthly activities for the last fiscal month—all data entry completed, bank statement reconciled, and accounting reports printed out.

2. Print out computer reports. You'll have to prepare the following reports for your accountant:

- Fiscal year Cash Report

- Fiscal year Profit and Loss Statement. Print out this report from Quicken

- Fiscal year Income and Expense Report. Print out this report from Quicken

3. Pull together all other necessary information. Your accountant will need asset information such as bank statements, capital equipment records, and accounts receivable (outstanding invoices) as well as liability information such as loan status and accounts payable. You may be asked to retrieve the weekly batched copies of jobs, monthly revenue and royalty reports, and other documents from your business files.

Renewing Insurance

When your insurance policies come up for renewal each year, you should review the coverage and premiums carefully. Sometimes, insurance companies will reduce coverage without your being aware of it. If any coverage has been reduced, ask your insurance agent to redo the policy and alert you to any changes in premiums. In reviewing your policies, you may notice that although the coverage remains the same, your insurance premiums have gone up. If that's the case, it pays to shop around for a better deal. Look elsewhere a different carrier.

CHAPTER 06

HIRING AND MANAGING EMPLOYEES

WHEN TO HIRE

Inspectors who run a business often wonder when to hire more inspectors. Before opening their business, some inspectors may decide to begin operations with a certain number of inspectors on board and then expand the staff as the business grows. Others may begin as a one-person operation and hire when the business expands beyond what they can handle.

A single inspector can perform about 400 inspections each year—roughly 2 a day, 5 days a week for 50 weeks. A general rule of thumb is to hire another inspector when the last inspector hired approaches 400 inspections.

If you're running a one-person home inspection business, you should start thinking about hiring a new inspector when you're doing about 40 inspections a month. You may want to wait until you're doing about 45 a month or even more. But be careful. You can spread yourself too thin. You may end up hiring under pressure, then continuing to handle the work load yourself while the inspector completes the training period.

The owner of a one-person inspection business may worry that there won't be enough business for another inspector. But a second inspector will provide twice the marketing power, which will bring in more customers.

This is a crucial point in the growth of a one-person company. There's no doubt that hiring your first inspector changes the nature of your day-to-day operations and results in other office issues. Some businesses may have a conflict at this time (for example, wanting to grow the business but not wanting the extra management tasks). This section provides the information you will need to hire and manage a staff of inspectors.

HIRING INSPECTORS

Some home inspection companies may have inspectors do inspections and nothing else. These companies are holding back their inspectors and are losing the potential inspectors have of making major contributions to the success of the business. Thinking of inspectors as "jobbers" can lead to hiring the wrong type of person. You should hire top-notch people and expect a lot out of them. Here's an overview of what the job entails:

- Inspections

- Handling of complaints

- Real estate agent marketing

- General business promotion

- Maintenance of professional standing

- Business development in some cases

Greater participation on the part of inspectors inspires a greater commitment to the success of your business.

Finding a Candidate

The best way to hire an inspector is by a referral from someone you know. Just getting the word out can result in a large number of candidates for the job. Realtors can be helpful because they generally know people in the homebuilding or home service trades. Some areas may have a fairly large number of people looking for work without the need to place ads. Electricians, carpenters, and a whole host of people associated with construction and home repair are aware that home inspection represents a good opportunity for them.

Moving forward, this chapter will discuss the hiring and training process for a new hire that is not already a trained and licensed (where applicable) home inspector. If possible, the first employee you hire should be someone with prior inspection experience.

Inspector Qualifications

Finding candidates is the easiest part of the hiring process. Finding the *right* candidate is harder. First, hold an image in your mind of the type of person you're looking for. You want a professional—a person with a professional appearance who can speak knowledgeably about technical matters, who is comfortable and confident with people, who makes a good impression with customers, and who real estate agents recognize as an equal.

Second, remember what the inspector's job entails. Ideally, you want a person who is well-rounded, one who can perform in a variety of situations—from doing quality inspections to making real estate agent presentations, and handling complaints. An inspector who has previous experience inspecting is a huge advantage.

Third, don't give up on finding the person who satisfies all of the job requirements. You'll find people who are technically astute but personally cold or who have great personalities but are unable to handle the technical aspects of the job. You don't want either type. Look for the person who combines people skills and technical capabilities. The qualifications you should insist on inspectors having are listed here in order of importance:

- **People skills.** This is the number one requirement. Everything else flows from the inspector's ability to communicate. An inspector should have a warm personality and genuinely enjoy people. A good inspector should be able to:

    —Convey a professional appearance and manner.

    —Communicate honestly, directly, and articulately using proper grammar.

    —Communicate technical subjects in simple ways.

—Inspire confidence in his or her abilities.

—Be sensitive to people and understand how people react to a situation.

—Engage in casual conversation and make people feel comfortable.

—Make a group presentation.

—Feel at ease in professional relationships.

—Treat people with genuine respect.

Technical aptitude: The second most important requirement is that the candidate have the potential of becoming an excellent inspector. It can be difficult to train inspectors in people skills if they don't have them naturally, but *AHIT* does know how to train people to become good inspectors (even when they have little technical background). However, candidates must have the aptitude in technical matters and the smarts for the job. Intelligence and the ability to learn are very important.

- **Technical background:** Preferably, the job candidate will have some background in the construction, repair, or maintenance trades or in related fields. Any knowledge and experience they have will be extremely useful to you and should be considered a plus. But surprisingly, *AHIT* puts technical background at the end of this list because it is possible to train the right person. If candidates have excellent people skills, intelligence, and technical aptitude but little previous experience, don't turn them away. *AHIT* will train them.

  The same is true for marketing and sales background. Any previous job experience in these areas should be considered a plus, but again, it's not necessary. The inspector training course at *AHIT* will cover these skills. Of course, finding a previously trained inspector will save you a great deal of time and money. However, you are better off hiring a newbie with all of the other skills mentioned than someone who is an inspector but lacks integrity or people skills.

  One other set of qualifications is important in a good inspector, and it falls under the general heading of character. It's not always easy to judge character when you're hiring an inspector. Sometimes, knowledge only comes after working with a person over time. Look for people with integrity, a strong work ethic, and ambition—people who work honestly and hard and who strive to achieve.

The Interview

You should interview each *good* candidate on two different occasions. Schedule the first interview in your office and weed out unacceptable candidates at that time. For those candidates with potential, schedule the second interview outside the office (at lunch perhaps) to observe the person in another environment.

Remember, as a business owner, you must maintain appropriate and professional hiring practices. Avoid potentially discriminating interview questions.

Matters of race, sex, age, and socioeconomic standing must not be discussed in the interview process.

Grade each candidate on the qualifications listed on the previous pages. Here are some suggestions for doing that during the interview:

- **Assess the candidate's people skills.** During the interview, keep the conversation flowing while you observe and ask yourself these questions: Is this person genuinely warm? How will he or she affect my customers? How would a real estate agent respond to this person? Is he or she a skilled communicator? A good listener? Responsive to what I'm saying? Do I instinctively dislike anything about him or her? Is the person too nervous for an interview situation? (You can expect the candidate to exhibit some nervousness but not an incapacitating amount.) Does the person make eye contact with me? If not, he or she may not be good in dealing with the public.

- **Test for technical aptitude.** Bring technical issues into the discussion and watch for the candidate's general level of interest and understanding. Ask the candidate about his or her experience with technical matters, related to either construction and home systems or some unrelated field. You may discover that the candidate's knowledge of construction is slim but that he or she can speak knowledgeably about computers or other technical areas. What you're looking for is intelligence and general aptitude for "difficult" subjects. Ask yourself: Does this person have an interest in technical subjects? Can this person speak intelligently about them? Seem to enjoy them? Seem willing to learn?

- **Explore the candidate's background.** Find out how much the candidate knows about construction and home systems. As was pointed out earlier, the candidate does not need to know everything an inspector must know, but you do want to get an understanding of the candidate's level of knowledge.

  Watch out for the candidate who tries to bluff his or her their way through this part of the interview. Ask direct questions about aspects of home inspection. The person you want to avoid hiring cannot admit his or her lack of knowledge about something and tends to say anything to cover it up. This should make you wary. Ask about the candidate's experience with marketing and sales and consider any experience a plus.

- **Review the candidate's writing skills.** Have the candidate fill out an application form.

  Review the form, assessing the candidate's writing skills, which are important in terms of report writing. Poor handwriting and bad spelling doesn't mean you should reject a good candidate. But if you do decide to hire someone with these shortcomings, you should mention that you expect him or her to improve these skills.

After you cover the points listed above, you should have a good idea of the person's people skills, technical aptitude, and background. Try to get a general feel about character. If everything checks out, you've got yourself a new inspector.

The Hiring Process
When you decide to hire someone for an inspector position, you'll be completing paperwork, asking the employee to fill in forms, and explaining several aspects of the job.

1. Have the employee sign the inspector contract. The document includes a noncompeting agreement and a confidentiality agreement.

2. Give the employee a copy of the job description and inspector classifications. It's important that employees understand up front what is required of them and how they may advance in the job.

3. Give the employee a policy handbook, reviewing the following:

   —Benefits, life and health insurance

   —Vacation

   —Sick time

   —Days off without pay

   —Holidays

   —Training period

   —Equipment requirements

   —Vehicle approval and standards

   —Promotional items

   —Memberships and affiliation

   —Handling of complaints

   —Confidentiality

4. Have the employee complete the necessary forms (for example, forms from the payroll company dealing with withholding as well as sign-up forms for life and health insurance).

5. Discuss what the training period will be like. A discussion of the inspector training program follows. The inspector should be fully informed about each aspect of it.

Initial Training

Each of your inspectors, whether employed at the start of your business or hired at a later date, should attend formal training. AHIT provides solid training and will work with you in developing successful inspectors for your company. Inspector education includes classroom studies, field training, and home study in the following aspects of home inspection:

- Home inspection history and purpose

- Association SOPs

- Inspector's Code of Ethics

- Performance of the home inspection, including:

  —Communications skills

  —Report writing

  —Salesmanship and marketing

- Technical instruction in the following:

  —Structural components

  —Exterior, roofing

  —Plumbing system

  —Electrical system

  —Heating system

  —Interiors

  —Insulation, ventilation

  —Environmental issues

  — Sales and marketing

  —Business operations

When newly trained inspectors return to you after completing the live training program, they should participate in your own local training before you send them out on inspections. This period can coincide with the inspector's completion of the *Home Study Master Course*. During this period, you may want new inspectors to accompany a working inspector on up to 20 inspections to observe and learn, then send a working inspector to observe and assist on the new inspector's first five jobs.

You may decide not to pay new inspectors during the training program or on the first 20 inspections. Each company should determine how it wants to handle this.

MANAGING INSPECTORS

Management is communication—verbal and written. Good management is continuous, effective communication. This section provides the information and tools necessary for managing inspectors.

The following five points are the crucial areas of communication that make up effective management.

1. Inform employees up front what is expected of them. Be clear on the legal agreement between your company and the inspectors, the requirements of the job, the requirements needed to advance in the job, and the policies that govern their employment. The following documents spell out what they need to know. Give them a copy of each:

   —Employment contract

   —Job description

   —Inspector classifications

   —Inspector Policy Handbook

2. Set goals for each inspector. Setting goals involves stating clearly what is expected, how much is expected, and by when it's expected. Make sure inspectors understand what those goals are.

3. Check inspectors' performance against their goals on an ongoing basis. Watch performance on a daily basis, keeping in mind how action today will affect the desired outcome six months down the road. Talk with inspectors about the job.

4. Give immediate feedback on performance. Praise good performance and correct errors in performance when they happen. Surprisingly, this is where most managers fail—ignoring inspectors when they do things right and not wanting to tell inspectors when they do something wrong.

5. Give annual written performance evaluations. For your records and for an "official" evaluation, schedule a meeting with each inspector to review last year's overall performance. This is an excellent time to set goals for the upcoming year. You may want to do this monthly or quarterly.

Setting Goals

When employees know exactly what is required of them, they tend to perform better. Nothing is worse for employees than not knowing and then being told later that they should have done their job this way. They're being treated unfairly.

Use the Inspector Performance Evaluation to set an employee's goals for the year. When you conduct a performance review at the end of the year, you'll use the same form. Both of you should be part of the process of setting goals. When the manager determines goals alone, they can be unrealistic with little chance of being met. On the other hand, employees may be tempted to set goals too low. By going through this process together and negotiating the goals, both of you should be satisfied. (Do *not* use the *General performance* or *Evaluation Comments* areas at this time.) Give the inspector a copy of the goals the two of you have set.

The Performance Evaluation states each element of the job description and provides room to write the goals. Goals may be numerical or may deal with general behaviors. Examples:

1. Perform buyer, seller, review, and additional inspections; write the appropriate reports; and indicate the follow-up that is needed for each inspection.

   Goals
   - *At seller inspections, promote the review inspection and get the buyer's name 50% of the time.*

   - *On opinion form statistics, rate over 90% on time and over 90% in response to first six questions dealing with satisfaction with inspection and inspector.*

   - *Improve handwriting.*

   - *Improve people skills.*

In the handling of customer complaints, you may want to set a minimum number of complaints as a goal or use a dollar amount paid out on claims.

Goals for the business element of a job description can be expressed in the number of inspections the inspector should generate in a subterritory for the next year (for example, 400) or as the total gross revenue expected from the subterritory in the next year ($100,000, for example).

For agent marketing, you might set a goal of scheduling and attending every real estate office meeting in your area for an entire year.

For the professional element of the job description, goals may be to become a member of a state or national association within the next year, to earn a certain number of MRCs (membership renewal credits), and to attend two seminars.

Evaluating Performance
At the end of the year, use the Performance Evaluation that was completed the previous year to review goals and performance with the inspector. Check off whether the inspector met his or her goals. The form has been designed this way for a reason. The check marks indicate whether the goals, as stated, were met. They don't necessarily mean pass/fail; there are too many mitigating circumstances. An inspector may not meet a goal because it was unrealistic to begin with. (You and the inspector may have missed the mark.)

However, there are general danger signs to watch for, and if you observe any, you need to discuss them with the inspector. Don't wait for the performance evaluation to raise these issues; as soon as you discover a problem, talk to the inspector about any behavior that he or she needs to correct. But if the behavior still persists at the annual meeting, discuss your concerns with the inspector, emphasizing that it must be corrected.

These are the danger signs to watch out for:

- Complaint calls and claims are unusually high for an inspector because of things done, not done, or missed during the inspection. You should deal with any big problems immediately. Analyze the complaints to see if the problem is sloppy work or a real deficiency in technical knowledge.

- Agents call you to complain about something the inspector did or didn't do or to express a general dissatisfaction with the way their client is treated.

- The opinion forms indicate that all of an inspector's inspections are taking less than one hour or between one and two hours. This is an indication that the inspector is rushing through the inspections, which should average about two hours each. Complaint calls are likely to be high for this inspector.

- The opinion forms indicate that the inspector is late for a good number of his or her inspections.

- The opinion forms indicate low satisfaction with the inspector on a specific point such as courtesy. Deal with this problem as soon as you notice it.

Use the *General performance area* for each job item to check whether you consider the inspector's performance to be excellent, satisfactory, or needs improvement. It's possible, although not probable, that each goal was missed yet you consider overall performance satisfactory. Use the *Evaluation comments* to indicate outstanding performance or needed improvement.

Set next year's or next quarter's goals at this meeting.

HIRING OFFICE STAFF

This section provides the information you'll need to hire and manage an office staff when you choose to do so. This section gives information for the following positions:

- A scheduler who answers the phones, deals with prospective customers, and closes the sale for you. This person also performs the daily activities described earlier—data entry, follow-up work, filing, ordering of supplies, etc.

- A bookkeeper who manages the financial and business accounting. This person performs most of the weekly, monthly, and yearly activities described –previously—managing the check register, reconciling Revenue and Cash Reports, producing payroll documentation, buying insurance, etc.

You don't need to fill both of these positions when you open your business, but the day will come when your business has grown to the point that you can afford your first staff member. By that time, you may be overwhelmed by the daily paperwork and data entry. You'll know when you reach that point, which is probably when you should consider hiring a scheduler. You may not need a bookkeeper on staff for a while because these activities are performed mostly at the end of each week, month, and year. But after you expand your inspector staff and take on the additional management tasks involved with them, you may want to pass along the paperwork to someone else. When your budget can afford it, you should think about hiring a bookkeeper. Or you may decide not to fill this position and, instead, hire a more highly qualified general manager to handle the entire business end of the operation and to manage employees.

Hiring office staff works best when you get a referral from someone you know. But you may want to place an ad on an online job board such as CareerBuilder or Monster.

The Hiring Process

When you decide to hire someone for an office staff position, you'll be completing paperwork, asking the employee to fill in forms, and explaining several aspects of the job.

1. Have the job candidate fill out an application form.

2. Have the employee sign the confidentiality agreement.

3. Give the employee a copy of the job description. It's important that employees understand up front what is required of them in the job.

4. Give the employee a policy handbook, reviewing the following:

    —Benefits, life and health insurance

    —Vacation

    —Sick time

    —Days off without pay

    —Holidays

    —Confidentiality

5. Have the employee complete the necessary forms (for example, forms from the payroll company dealing with withholding as well as sign-up forms for life and health insurance).

Scheduler Qualifications

It's vital that you hire the right person for this position. This employee will be responsible for capturing appointments for you and will be the voice of your business. He or she should meet the following qualifications:

- **People skills.** This is the number one requirement. Success in this position depends on the person's phone skills. A scheduler should have a warm personality and genuinely enjoy talking to people. A good scheduler should be able to:

—Transmit a professional impression.

—Transmit a genuine desire to serve callers.

—Communicate honestly, directly, and articulately using proper grammar.

—Inspire confidence in the company's services.

—Be patient with people and treat them with respect.

—Speak knowledgeably about home inspection.

—Ask for the sale.

- **Ability to learn.** The candidate for the scheduler's job must learn about the subject of home inspection and speak knowledgeably about it with customers. Look for intelligence in a scheduler. And because the scheduler is going to be stating prices on the phone, look for someone with math skills.

- **Organizational skills.** The scheduler will be responsible for the day-to-day operations of the office, managing schedules, your files, and supplies—important tasks that keep the office running smoothly. You want someone who can work independently. Look for a person who enjoys taking responsibility for these types of tasks and likes keeping things in order. Previous experience should be considered a plus.

- **Office background.** You'll want to hire a scheduler who comes with a set of office skills so that he or she can pick up the work quickly. These skills include data entry; familiarity with computers; and knowledge of database and word processing software, fax machines, and copiers.

Scheduler Training
The inspector should put a new scheduler through a rigorous training program. The first step is to take the scheduler along on at least two inspections so that he or she can experience a home inspection first-hand. Phone training is critical and is included in this manual.

Bookkeeper Training
Each new office staff member should accompany a working inspector on at least two inspections. Even the bookkeeper, who has little customer contact on a routine basis, will better understand the business after seeing an inspector in action.

Ongoing Management
Management of the office staff doesn't differ in principle from managing inspectors. The following activities are required with office staff as well:

- Inform employees up front what is expected of them. When they are hired, give them their job description and the Office Staff Policy Handbook.

- Set goals for the office staff.

- Check performance against goals regularly.

- Give immediate feedback on performance.

- Give annual written performance evaluations and salary reviews.

Use a Scheduler and/or Bookkeeper Performance Evaluation to set the employee's goals for the year. When you conduct a performance review at the end of the year, you'll use the same form. Both of you should be part of the process of setting goals. By going through this process together and negotiating the goals, both of you should be satisfied. Give the employee a copy of the goals the two of you have set.

The Performance Evaluation states each element of the job description and provides room to write the goals. Goals may be numerical or may deal with general behaviors. Here's an example.

Answer the phone, fill in appointment sheets, determine inspection prices, and schedule appointments.

Goals:

—Close 80% of incoming calls.

—Reach 95% accuracy in setting inspection prices.

—Improve on scheduling conflicts.

For tasks such as entering data, posting schedules, and performing follow-up work, you may want to set time goals (for example, all data entry completed by the end of each working day; next day's schedule posted by 5 p.m.) or accuracy goals.

At the end of the year, use the Performance Evaluation that was completed the previous year to review goals and performance with the employee. Check off whether the employee met his or her goals.

There are danger signs to watch for, and if you observe any, you need to discuss them with the scheduler. Don't wait until the annual performance review to point out these deficiencies; as soon as you discover a problem, talk to the scheduler about what he or she needs to correct.

These are the danger signs to watch for:

- **The statistics show a dropping close rate on incoming calls.** Have the scheduler use a call tracking method to indicate the number of incoming calls and those that close.

  Although you can't always attribute a high close rate entirely to scheduler performance (it might be the result of good agent marketing), a dropping close rate is usually the scheduler's fault. You need to deal with this problem right away. Listen to some scheduler calls to see if something can be corrected. It is possible for a scheduler to increase his or her close rate 10% just by saying, for example, "We can schedule this appointment tomorrow at 10" instead of asking if the customer would like to schedule an appointment.

- **You find too many database entry errors when you're pulling weekly reports.** Accuracy in database entry is important to your business. You should tell a scheduler immediately about the type of errors that are occurring and ask him or her to improve.

- **The office runs out of supplies.** This is particularly serious when you run out of *Property Inspection Reports* and other supplies you must have. Managing the inventory of office supplies is no easy task, and the scheduler must make every effort to become familiar with the flow of supplies so that he or she can plan ahead on reordering. Work with the scheduler to correct problems in this area.

After reviewing goals with the scheduler, indicate whether you consider the employee's performance to be excellent, satisfactory, or needs improvement. Use *Evaluation Comments* to indicate outstanding performance or needed improvement.

Use this annual performance evaluation to review salary with office staff, giving raises at this time. Also use the meeting to set next year's goals.

BEING A MANAGER

You already learned what's involved in hiring and managing employees. But who is going to provide the kind of people management that will make your business a success? You are. People management is an art form with guiding principles so simple that most people aren't aware of them.

Principle 1: Before you became a people manger, you were a human being. Once you become a manager, strive to remain a human being. Not much else is required of you.

Some people have an image of an old-time, autocratic boss, and they take on these characteristics when they start to manage people. They're the type of supervisor who doesn't share information with employees, then becomes angry when employees don't do what's required. Or they manage by intimidation and blow up and cause a great deal of discord. Another type of manager with whom people are familiar is the arrogant one who sneers at anything underlings suggest. This person believes that he or she has is better than anyone else. That's not true. Sometimes, people who take on people management responsibilities forget everything they know about dealing with people. They forget how to be human beings. It would behoove you to remain the same person people have grown to know and love.

Principle 2: Tell employees what is expected of them. Don't be surprised when they do it.

We have already discussed job descriptions and goals. This information is not just paperwork—it state in fairly precise terms what you expect inspectors and office staff to do for your business. Employees need to know their job descriptions and goals so that they can focus and plan how they're going to accomplish what you've asked. With this knowledge, employees have the tools they need to succeed in the job.

Principle 3: Employees are adults and can think for themselves. They may need your help once in a while, but not all the time.

Nothing's worse than a manager who oversees an employee's work when it's not necessary. Some managers are compulsive on this point, needing to be "all over" an employee all the time. The mistake in this instance is that the manager doesn't see that the employee *is* doing the job—and would probably do the job better without so much interference.

You should manage closely when an employee is new on the job and, when he or she is performing to your satisfaction, get out of the way. There are ways to check an employee's performance without being a pest. Create an atmosphere where employees come to you when they need help and then help them. But don't punish them for needing it.

Principle 4: Give your employees feedback. Praise what's right and correct what's wrong as soon as you notice it.

Simple? Not really. Most managers fail to give feedback to employees in any helpful way. Managers may make two mistakes. The first mistake is to forget to give praise when they see someone doing something right. Often, the best performers get the least praise because managers think they must know how valued they are. Not so. All employees need to be told when they're doing something right and be praised for it. This is not just feel-good management. This is checking performance against goals on an ongoing basis, letting employees know they're meeting the standards.

The second mistake many managers make is to notice someone doing something wrong but not mentioning it. Instead, they hold it in and become frustrated with an employee over a long period of time until it finally blows up. Then the employee will probably ask, "Why didn't you tell me?" Why, indeed?

When an employee makes a mistake, talk to them as soon as you notice it. Tell them what the mistake was and ask them to correct it. Be direct and brief. An employee needs to know what's wrong so that he or she can avoid making the mistake again.

It should be that simple. But for some reason there are managers who can't mention what's wrong without insulting the employee. That's feel-bad management. Your purpose in correcting employee behavior is not to make employees suffer. It's to ensure that they stop making the mistake and still feel good about themselves.

CHAPTER 07
WEBSITES, ELECTRONIC AND SOCIAL MEDIA MARKETING

WHY BUILD A WEBSITE?

As you begin to build your brand and marketing strategies, there is one piece of the puzzle you cannot skip—creating a website for your business. While this is generally true for any business in this day and age, it is especially important in the home inspection industry for a few key reasons.

First, using the Internet, you can market to all of your prospective clients at one time. NAR's 2014 Profile of Home Buyers and Sellers state that nearly all (92%) homebuyers, your primary clients, use the Internet when looking for homes and working through the home buying process. The key to effective marketing is to put your message in front of as many prospects as possible. Leveraging a website will allow you to put this message in front of thousands of homebuyers/sellers in your area. Your website will be the foundation of all of your digital marketing efforts moving forward. Any form of online advertising or marketing will direct prospective clients to your website. Although print marketing (brochures, postcards, etc.) are still an integral part of your marketing strategy, a strong digital presence will provide the best return on your marketing investments.

Second, the home inspection industry is different from many service industries in that your prospective clients will hire you before ever meeting you. By the time you show up to an inspection, the homebuyer or seller has already selected your company. Because of this, effective marketing is more important than salesmanship. Salesmanship is the key when a homebuyer calls your office. However, that person will never find his or her way to your phone or office without effective marketing to direct them there. And if you have done your job correctly, you won't need a hard sale over the phone because your website has effectively sold your services to the client before he or she picks up the phone.

GET A DOMAIN NAME

The first step in creating your website is to find or create your domain name. Your domain name is not only the address of your website, but also the first tool in your digital marketing arsenal. You want to find a website name that represents your business accurately. A great way to start is by doing a generic search of your business name or using a domain name registrar such as GoDaddy.com or whoIs.com. If the domain name for your business is available (for example, ABCinspections.com), buy it! If it isn't, you have a few options: Come up with a new domain name or try to purchase that one.

If the first domain name you want is taken, don't fret. Look for available domain names that are more specific to your location or use a hyphen. For example, if ABCinspections.com and ABChomeinspections.com are taken by a company in California and your business is located in Georgia, try something like ABCgeorgiainspections.com or ABC-inspections.com.

If you have your heart set on a certain domain name, you always have the option of purchasing the address from the current owner. That being said, this process will be more expensive than purchasing a new name. The first thing you must do is find the registered owner of the website. You can do this using a service such as who.is (https://who.is). When you find the owner, call or email the person to ask if the site is for sale. If he or she is interested in hearing your offer, make one. Remember, this is a negotiation—just like buying property.

Aside from purchasing your main address, you will also want to purchase a few more addresses to redirect traffic back to your main address. A great place to start is by purchasing any names with typos that users may enter when looking for your website. Purchase as many of these as are available for a low cost. Also, you may want to purchase other domains that will be effective in marketing your brand. For example, if your business is based in Canton, Georgia, you may want to purchase available domains such as CantonHomeInspections.com, GeorgiaHomeInspections.com, and NorthGAInspections.com. This serves two purposes: By redirecting those links to your site, you will drive more traffic and search results to your domains and you can prevent future competition from using these names.

When you have purchased the right domain name and all other relevant variations, purchase the longest registration period that is available and make sure you remember the date your registration will expire. If you accidentally allow your registration to lapse, there may be negative consequences, ranging from losing a few days of traffic to having your domain name purchased right under your nose and held ransom by a domain squatter. Yes, this is a real concern; it has happened to organizations as reputable as the Dallas Cowboys football team.

HIRE A WEB DESIGNER

As stated earlier, your company's website will be the cornerstone of your digital marketing efforts. The majority of your prospective clients will look to your website and make assumptions about your credibility, professionalism, experience, and quality of work based on what they find. With this in mind, you should hire a professional to design, build, and maintain your website so that its design is streamlined and professional and its functionality is free of bugs and other problems.

When looking for someone to build your website, you have many options. AHIT works with a company that will build your website and specializes in sites for home inspectors. A quick online search will bring thousands of results ranging from enterprise development agencies to college students looking to make some money on the side. Find a web developer/designer that specializes in building websites for small businesses and has a proven track record of quality work. You do not want to be the first website this person or company has built. Find someone who understands your industry and the goals of your website. If he or she has built home inspection websites before, that is a definite plus. A very important consideration is to find someone with whom you enjoy speaking and working. While your website is being built, you will have to work with the builder closely to ensure that your company is being represented at the highest level. This may include making hundreds of subtle changes along the way. Work with someone you believe you can trust to make your vision come true. Communication is the key in building the "perfect" website. Make sure you can communicate effectively with whoever is doing the job.

YOUR WEBSITE'S SINGLE OBJECTIVE

Once you have successfully registered your domain names and found the right person or organization to build your website, it is time to begin working with the designer. Every great design is made possible with a clear, agreed-upon objective. Many of the websites you visit may have a few objectives, such as providing interesting content, processing orders, and driving repeat visits. However, home inspection websites serve a single purpose—to drive sales. More specifically, you want your website to drive users to contact your office to hire you for a job or at least to get them to call your office to get an estimate and be sold on why your service is best.

To this end, you should keep a few key things in mind. First, you must understand who your customer is. The vast majority of people hire a home inspector only once every several years. Chances are very high that once they leave your website, they will not return. For this reason, every page on your website must give them what they want and do so quickly. You should consider every page on your website as a sales pitch. Do not take up precious space on your page to sell items, to post about your business needs (for example, job openings), or anything else that takes away from the main goal. Second, every page should have at least one (preferably many) clear calls to action, such as "Call me now" and "Book an Inspection today" and should clearly outline why your services are best for the client. Any page that discusses additional inspection services should explain why the client will have the best experience with your company and how you provide these services in a way that sets you apart from the competition.

As the discussion continues on how to create the component parts of your website, you must remember this central goal. It is very easy to get caught up in the details of design, such as color schemes, pictures, and fonts, and lose sight of your central goal: to provide the information that is needed to sell yourself and your services. When in doubt, keep the website simple and clearly define your values.

DESIGNING YOUR HOME PAGE

Most, if not all, of the traffic on your website will end up on your home page first. The second a user sees your home page is the most crucial moment in your potential relationship. The user will not take time to read all of the content on your site; he or she will simply scan your home page and decide whether to continue reading or find another home inspector.

The easiest way to ensure that users stay on your website is to give them what they want and to provide it quickly. If a potential client has found his or her way to your website, there is only one thing the person is looking for: to hire a great home inspector. Provide that. Prospective clients need to know that your home page has exactly what they are looking for or is, at most, a click away.

Your home page should include the following:

—Your company logo, at the top and larger than anything else

—Your company tagline

—Easy site navigation (which we will discuss later)

—A snapshot of reasons you are the most qualified (organization memberships, awards, certifications, etc.),

—Your USPs

—A snapshot of the services you offer

—Locations that you serve

—Additional information that the customer will find useful

One effective way to do this is to include a brief promotional video that outlines the facts on your home page. This is included with your AHIT website. This works well because it is the quickest way to communicate the information, it takes little effort on the part of the client, and it will increase the popularity of your website.

Along with a video, pictures are an effective way to persuade people to research your company further. However, you must be careful when using pictures. If a picture is worth a thousand words, make sure it tells the story you want to be told. Avoid stock photos and any other photos that don't convey a clear message. For example, a photo of a random house says nothing. However, a photo of you in the field can show your style of work. A photo of you and your vehicle can show that you use quality instruments and take pride in your work (assuming that your truck is in good shape). A photo of your team at a local landmark tells visitors that you are a local business, and people like to shop locally. Overall, remember that every photo on your page must be intentional and useful.

WEBSITE NAVIGATION

Once you build your home page, it is time to begin working on the rest of your website. To start mapping out this process, you should define your site's navigation. Easy and user-friendly navigation should be a priority in your design. Visitors to your website are accustomed to easy navigation and will quickly turn to a new website if they can't find what they want within a few clicks.

To avoid "banner blindness," you should place links to additional pages vertically in the left border of the home page. This is proven to draw a reader's attention to those links, and the vertical orientation implies hierarchy. Leverage this hierarchy to direct users to the information you want them to see.

Here are some pages you should consider adding to your site:

- Home page

- Residential Home Inspections

  ○ Outline what is covered in your home inspections (for example, Roofing, Plumbing, and Mechanical and Structural Items).

- Additional Inspections

  ○ Include information about the critical problems you are solving with your additional inspection services.

- Why Hire Me?

  - Don't be shy! Include information about your experience, certifications, USPs, and superior customer service.

- Standards of Practice

- My Promise to You!

  - This is similar to the "Why Hire Me?" section. However, use this page to include a personal note to potential clients.

- Reviews

  - Leverage tools such as the Better Business Bureau and Yelp, to build a library of positive reviews. This will help give your prospects peace of mind.

- How-to articles

  - Basic how-to articles can show that you have expertise, experience, and tools that your competition lacks. Most importantly, this can be very useful in Search Engine Optimization (to be discussed later.)

- Contact Me!

These suggestions are standard. If you want to include additional pages, feel free to do so. However, keep the central goal of the website in mind when considering this.

DESIGNING ADDITIONAL PAGES

Once an outline of general content and navigation hierarchy has been created, it is time to design the individual pages that go with it. It is critical that you keep the same general principles in mind when designing these pages as you did when working on the home page.

- Each page is a billboard. Do not include so much information that the reader is overwhelmed with text. Be deliberate in your use of words, pictures, and videos. Make sure everything you add is driving the user to a decision.

- On every page and in central view, include clear calls to action. This is often best achieved with an action button ("Schedule an Inspection Today," "Call Me Now," "Find My Contact Info," etc.)

  - Ideally, these will bring the user to a page that contains your contact information so that he or she can call you. This link also should include a basic form, allowing the prospect to submit his or her contact information and the best time for you to call.

  - As your business grows to several inspectors, you may want to use an online scheduling tool that allows homeowners to schedule an inspection from your website. However, you shouldn't do this at the start of your business because there is no substitute for great salesmanship on the phone. In addition, you don't want prospects to see when your schedule is light, which implies that you aren't getting much work because you aren't the best.

- ○ Also, if you plan to market heavily to real estate agents, you should consider adding a button that allows them to refer their clients to your website. This can be as simple as providing them with a link to your contact information.

- You cannot overlook your spelling, grammar, and writing skills. People are going to hire you to inspect their homes and write a report about it. If your website does not show that you are a master of the written word, why should they trust you to write a report for them?

ONGOING WEBSITE MANAGEMENT

With the principles outlined previously, you should have enough information to build the first version of your website. However, many small businesses have a bad habit of not revisiting their website once this stage is complete. Don't do that. Your website should be a living document that is constantly updated and fine-tuned to achieve a maximum return on your investment. You should maintain a relationship with the person or company who built your website and, if he or she does not want the work, you can hire a webmaster to keep the site running. Once you start driving decent traffic to your page, if your website is down for even a day, you can suffer serious losses.

Looking at Basic Website Metrics and Conversion Rates

Free tools such as Google Analytics provide you with metrics used to judge the performance of your website. For example:

- The amount of traffic you receive

- How long users stay on your website

- How many pages they visit

- Where they go after visiting your website

- Where they find your website

- How many are submitting forms

- General location of your visitors

- Gender of your visitors

In the beginning stages of your online marketing career, these metrics may be a bit daunting. So let's focus on some key conversion rates that you should keep in mind. At the most basic level, you need to focus on three things:

1. How much traffic you generate

2. What percentage of those people contact you

3. Of the ones you contact, how many schedule an inspection

The last metric is most highly affected by your phone skills. However, it is crucial to keep it in mind when looking at your website. For example, if you generate 1000 unique visits per month, 3% of the people who visit your website contact you, and of those that contact you, one-third book an inspection, you will get 10 inspections a month from your website $(1000 \times 0.03 \times 0.33 = 10)$.

This is where playing with your website can become fun. Assuming that you were to increase each of those metrics by one-third, you could increase your monthly inspections by 120% $(1300 \times 0.04 \times .43 = $ approximately 22 inspections a month). As you can see, minor changes to the website can yield huge results.

When looking at these basic metrics, it becomes clear how the pieces of information described earlier become helpful. For example, if you want to increase the rate at which people are contacting you, look at who is coming to your website. If the majority of your visitors are women, try making adjustments that are geared more toward women. If you find that the majority of your visitors come from a specific part of your territory, include a page that is geared toward that demographic. As you begin to collect this data, you should be making slight tweaks to your website to improve the three main data points used in the previous examples.

SEARCH ENGINE OPTIMIZATION (SEO)

If you have a website, hardly a week will pass without spam appearing in your inbox, promising you a page one Google spot; just delete it. The fact that the first page of results for any search has limited space and only a few pages will get on it—unless they pay to do so. There are, however, some things you can do to help people find your website.

Get listed on your inspector association "Find an Inspector" function Inspector association websites such as ASHI and InterNACHI often appear near the top of search results. From there, people can enter location information and get a list of nearby member inspectors. This is one benefit of belonging to an inspector association, and the membership fee is usually more than paid for by referrals you will get from the association website. Don't forget to get listed on the local association chapter website too.

Don't waste this benefit. You should keep your listing current. You should take time to make your listing stand out from that of other members. Make sure you list all your credentials and write a company description that makes people want to call you instead of another member.

Expand your search term potential The results from someone's search query often match the exact words used in the query. The query "Raleigh home inspectors" is a different query from "Raleigh home inspector." Search engines return results based to a large extent on the keywords or phrases attached to your website pages, and the search engine sees only about five such keywords or phrases. So how do you get more of these important keywords or phrases?

Getting more websites is one answer. They need to be different websites; a slight difference will do. Otherwise, the search engine will lower the ranking for all your websites. Use different keywords or phrases for each website to expand the potential for showing up on a search.

Create spider-friendly website pages Search engines read websites using programs called spiders. Spiders are programmed to read a limited number of website items and to ignore everything else. For example, spiders read only text. They don't read pictures or graphics. So if the only time your company name or location appears on a web page is in a picture, a logo, or something similar, the spider won't read it and your website probably won't show up on a search. Your webmaster should be optimizing your website as part of his or her service. You might ask what he or she is doing to improve your website ranking. If you create your own website, you need to know search engine optimization techniques. Plenty of resources on the Internet can help you with this.

Got links? Search engines like links to other websites, especially inbound links to your website. Inbound links make your website seem more worthy of attention and thus worthy of a higher ranking. Exchanging links with inspectors in other markets is a good way to get inbound links. As is true for all links, try to embed a keyword in the link. For example, the company name Dream Home Consultants would not be a very good inbound link. *Home* is the only keyword, and it is fairly generic. *Dream Home Inspection* would be a better link. *Home inspection* is a good keyword. The best link would be *Raleigh Home Inspection*. That's a phrase that someone would enter as a search term.

Pay someone to do it In today's online marketplace, it is easy to pay an organization, often the one that built your initial website, a monthly fee to manages your search engine efforts. Often, if the fee is right, this is money well spent.

GOOGLE ADWORDS

You have probably seen search results at the top and down the right side of a Google search result. These are called pay-per-click ads. The advertiser pays only when someone clicks the ad. Google AdWords, an online advertising service, campaigns can be an effective strategy to gain customers. The general goal of Adwords is not simply to drive traffic to your website, but to drive qualified traffic from visitors who are likely to want your inspection services. Here are some suggested keywords:

- Your name

- Your company name

- Your town/city

- The regional areas that you service

- The services you provide

It is vital that you keep track of your AdWords investment and make sure you are making more money than you are spending (and that you do some basic math to decide what daily spending limits to set for yourself).

A FINAL WORD ON DIGITAL INVESTMENTS

Once you have built a website successfully, you will gain the attention not only of prospective clients, but also of different marketing agencies in your area. Do not be alarmed when you begin receiving emails from vendors claiming that they can boost your SEO efforts, online traffic, conversions, etc.

When evaluating different vendors and marketing strategies, you need to keep one thing in mind: return on investment (ROI). In other words, how much money will you be bringing in if you spend some cash on this investment? Whenever you are deciding whether to invest in a new service (including the ones discussed previously), ask yourself (or the vendor), "What ROI can I expect to see?" In the early stages of your business, you should invest only in practices that you are confident will generate a 4:1 ROI or higher.

For example, you are looking at a digital agency to manage your SEO efforts. Currently, you have 1000 monthly hits, 3% contact you, and 33% of those contacts book inspections (10 inspections per month). With the new agency, you are confident it will be able to increase traffic by 50%. If your other metrics stay the same, this will result in about five more inspections a month ($1500 \times 0.03 \times 0.33 = 14.9$). If the monthly cost of this service is approximately equal to the price of one inspection, this is a great investment with a 5:1 ROI. If the agency will be charging you thousands of dollars a month, this is not a sound investment. It is through this lens that you should view all potential online investments. Any skilled and successful marketer who is soliciting you also should be able to discuss the investment in these terms. If you are speaking with someone who does not seem comfortable working like this, that person may not be very good at his or her job and you should look elsewhere.

WEBSITE SUMMARY

- Overall, there are many things to consider when building a website. However, building the website itself is not something you should skimp on. It will become the central marketing hub for your business. All of your brochures, business cards, etc., will include a link to the site.

- Chances are high that you are not a website developer. Hire one you trust and can communicate with effectively.

- Your website has one purpose: to sell home inspections. Do not waste valuable online real estate with items that take away from this goal.

- Keep an eye on relevant website metrics and continuously aim to increase conversion rates.

- Investments in your website are the key. However, always keep one thing in mind when doing so: ROI.

The average age of a home inspector is in the fifties. Many people around this age find social media to be a little silly. Some of it is silly, but this medium can have a serious business purpose if you use it wisely. The business purposes of social media is to have your name in front of homebuyers, real estate agents, and other contacts when they are ready to purchase an inspection or refer you to someone who is.

Most people are in the market for a home inspection a few days every few years. If your name is in front of them when they are ready (or when someone they know is ready), then at least you should be one of the inspectors they call. You may be the only inspector they call if you have done a good job using social media.

Two major social networks are most beneficial in growing your business: Facebook and LinkedIn. By now, you are probably familiar with Facebook. With over one billion users a month, Facebook has become a networking and advertising gold mine in global and local markets. LinkedIn, on the other hand, is a slightly more specific social network whose aim is to connect businesspeople. LinkedIn provides an avenue for home inspectors to establish credibility with regard to their professional identity and to demonstrate their subject matter expertise.

This section will discuss some of the most effective free ways to drive business via social media.

CREATING AND GROWING YOUR SOCIAL MEDIA PROFILES

This section begins with an important warning that applies to everything you post on the Internet whether the post is to social media, a blog, or your website. Be careful with your posts. Once they're out there, they're out there forever. Never post anything that could detract, even a little, from your professional image. If you wouldn't want your mother, wife, or minister to see it, don't post it.

You will want to create two types of profiles on these networks—a personal page and a business page. Your personal page refers to yourself directly, not to your business. You may already have a Facebook page that you use to connect with family and friends. Depending on the content you publish, this can be a useful avenue for creating more personal relationships with certain business contacts—generally, those people whom you have known for a long time and are open to having a personal relationship with. Because the majority of your business will come from referrals, building these relationships can be very beneficial.

Your personal LinkedIn profile is an entirely different story, however. The key is to set it up as an online resume with a professional photograph. Include awards, certifications, and professional group memberships in the profile. Making your headline a catchy tagline or call to action, like you often see on business cards, is powerful. The goal of your LinkedIn profile is to connect with all of your business contacts and to make new ones. By joining groups, participating in comment threads, and asking for introductions, you can easily grow your professional network to include hundreds of relevant business contacts in your area. By posting relevant business articles, notes about your business, or fun things such as crazy inspection findings, you can keep yourself—and ultimately your inspection business—in the minds of your growing business network.

Along with your personal profiles, you must create business profiles on these networks. In general, your business profiles should include all relevant contact information, your logos and brandings, and information about why people should choose your business over the competition. This includes the USPs that were discussed earlier. Like you did with your personal LinkedIn page, you should post content that is relevant to your business and to those who are looking to promote your business to their clients and friends.

With regard to the business page, there is one main difference between Facebook and LinkedIn: "likes." Your goal as a business owner on LinkedIn is to provide business information and post relevant content. You do the same on Facebook, but your ultimate goal is to get "likes."

What are Facebook "likes," and why are they important? A Facebook "like" is a voluntary action that Facebook users can take to show that they recommend your business or, at least, to recommend that their Facebook network view your page. "Likes" are important because they can grow your sphere of influence on Facebook dramatically.

When someone "likes" your page, it ensures that a large number of your posts will be shown directly to the person via his or her feed. This will drive interaction and engagement on your page. More importantly, when a user "likes" and interacts on Facebook, your business will be promoted in the feed of his or her network. This is how people who have never been introduced to your brand learn about your page and business. In short, capturing "likes" will keep in the minds of those who follow you and introduce your business to all of their friends.

JOINING GROUPS

One additional way to grow your social presence is by creating, joining, and participating in Facebook and LinkedIn groups. Groups allow people with common interests or affiliations to come together and interact online. First, you should consider joining all professional groups that are relevant to you and your clients. This may include communities of inspectors such as ASHI and InterNACHI and real estate associations. You should join both national and local groups. Second, search for groups that are likely to include prospective homebuyers in your area.

Once you have joined these groups, don't be shy. If you want people to see you, you must post, comment, and interact. If you have designed your profiles as described above, you should want to show them off. Remember, your goal is grow your network and direct traffic to your page, website, and office. The best way to drive these metrics is to post items that provide value that is relevant to whoever is in your group. For example, you shouldn't post a topic such as "Five Great Tips for Moving Your Home" to a group of inspectors. However, you should post that to a group of homebuyers or homeowners in your area.

CHAPTER 08

THE INSPECTION PLAN

INSPECTION CONTENT AND STANDARDS

The general home inspection includes inspecting the following aspects of the home:

- **Landscaping**—its effects on the foundation

- **Siding, trim, exterior windows and storms**—the general condition of each

- **Roof, chimney, flashings, valleys**—evidence of water penetration, materials, condition

- **Gutters, downspouts**—general condition, effects of dampness in basement, ability to carry off rainwater

- **Driveways, patios, decks, porches**—general condition of each

- **Air conditioner compressor**

- **Walls, floors, ceilings, interior windows**—general condition of each

- **Plumbing systems**—all visible fixtures, pipes and drains tested for operation

- **Electrical systems**—outside entrance wiring, service panel, visible wiring inspected; random testing of outlets

- **Heating system**—visible portion of heating plant and components

- **Attic**—visible roof sheathing, ventilation, insulation, framing

- **Basement or crawlspace**—soundness of foundation, evidence of moisture

Back in 1976, home inspections were not very thorough and were not very well defined. Aware of the need for standards in the industry, a group of inspectors formed a professional organization that year—the American Society of Home Inspectors, or ASHI. Over time, ASHI defined the home inspection process and developed SOPs and a code of ethics for its members. Since then, many state and national societies and associations have been formed, and they work together to maintain the standards of home inspection, including NAHI and InterNACHI. Do some online research to find the inspection association that fits you best. You should become a member of many associations, giving you the opportunity to benefit from the values that each provides.

NOTE: It's important to note the difference between a general inspection and a technically exhaustive inspection. A technically exhaustive inspection is an in-depth inspection of each component of a property that is completed by a certified or licensed individual for each component; experts such as electricians, plumbers, structural engineers, and roofers are used. This type of inspection is far more costly than the general type.

CODE OF ETHICS

Honesty, morality, and integrity should form the foundation of ethics under which all inspectors work.

- **Maintain professional standards.** A successful business is built on reputation, and a good reputation is built on quality performance and ethical standards.

- **Uphold the honor and integrity of the home inspection profession.** The industry survives on the trust of its customers and referral base. Trust, honesty and professionalism is the foundation of your business

- **Avoid any apparent conflicts of interest.** Be aware of the type of situation that constitutes a conflict of interest. Remain free of entanglements to ensure that the client receives an objective and impartial inspection.

Some examples of conflicts of interest are as follows:

- You have a financial interest in the property under inspection. That is, if you're the owner or partial owner of the home being inspected, it's an obvious conflict of interest and a difficult, if not impossible, situation in which to render an unbiased opinion. Don't do these inspections.

- You are inspecting the home of a relative or close personal friend that's for sale. Here, there's a conflict of interest because you may have a problem rendering an unfavorable opinion to your relative or friend.

- The agent is a relative or close personal friend. Again, the conflict of interest is apparent because you want to avoid damaging the pending transaction for the agent's sake. You should avoid this situation.

- You have a financial relationship with the agent, which is a gross conflict of interest.

- You have a financial relationship with a contracting firm such as a plumbing, heating, electrical, or roofing company. The conflict of interest is obvious. Giving impartial opinions on the condition of a home's systems is impossible if your end goal is to refer repair work to your own firm.

- **Disclose to clients immediately any potential conflicts of interest.** Sometimes, when you know a large number of people in your community, conflicts of interest can't be avoided. In those cases, be honest about any relationship you have with the parties involved in inspections and tell clients before you take the job. Let them decide whether to hire you.

- **Give educated opinions on subjects you know; do not guess about any situation.** Don't express opinions about situations you're not familiar or experienced with. If you start guessing about things you don't know, you may be giving inaccurate information that can result in a lawsuit. Be aware of the limits of your training and knowledge and don't comment outside the stated purpose of the inspection. In addition, don't make decisions for clients or advise them about whether they should or shouldn't buy a property.

- **Be unbiased and communicate all findings in a proper and honest manner.** Communication of the inspection findings is just as important as the inspection itself. Report what you find honestly and clearly, free of personal bias. Be sensitive to what your customers understand when you're talking to them and take responsibility for that understanding. Patiently repeating important information can protect you from future lawsuits.

- **Hold information in confidence for the client; do not reveal information unless approved by the client or unless required by law.** Make sure your customer checks "Yes" or "No" to the statement "Client agrees to release reports to seller/buyer/agent" on the Preinspection Agreement. If "No" is checked, honor that by not discussing inspection findings in front of the agent or other parties not designated by the client.

- **Do not profit in any manner from commissions or allowances given by outside parties.** See the examples of conflicts of interest stated earlier.

- **Do not perform any other work on an inspected home other than future home inspections; an inspection cannot be used as a way to obtain repair or related work on the house.** This rule and the one above must be followed to ensure that you maintain the professionalism and integrity of the home inspection profession. (See the examples of conflicts of interest provided earlier.)

- **Become a better inspector and maintain certifications.** It's important to remain up-to-date with the latest in building technology and materials and to keep your professional skills sharp.

THE INSPECTOR CODE OF ETHICS

Trust, honesty, and professionalism should form the foundation of ethics under which all inspectors work.

- Follow the code of ethics.

- Be professional in dress and appearance. Being a professional, a home inspector should dress accordingly. In your area, this may mean a shirt and tie, but a fashionable casual pullover shirt or sweater and casual pants are fine if the image is a professional one. Inspectors must establish themselves as peers of customers. Wash-and-wear clothes and a washable raincoat or jacket are best because they are easy to keep clean. Leather shoes with rubber soles (for safety on the roof) are appropriate; sneakers and jeans are not. Coveralls worn in crawl spaces and for basement inspection can get dirty and should be washed regularly.

- Be professional in customer relationships. The code of ethics lays the ethical foundation of customer relationships.

  —Honesty, integrity, and complete impartiality are vital. Beyond the moral reasons for professional behavior, each inspector should cultivate the people skills of putting people at ease, be knowledgeable and helpful, and avoid being adversarial with any parties present at the inspection.

- **Develop excellent communication skills.** The home inspection business *is* communication. An inspector's social conversations, discussions of the Preinspection Agreement, explanations, and discussions of findings are important aspects of the job. Each inspector should strive to communicate clearly and sincerely and in a friendly manner.

- **Develop excellent report-writing skills.** Not everyone has good handwriting, is a good speller, and writes using perfect English. But the customer must be able to read and understand the *Property Inspection Report*. Each inspector should make sure he or she has the skills needed to write clear, precise reports. A well-written report that documents *all* findings will prevent future problems if a complaint or claim comes up. Remember, if it isn't in the report, it didn't happen.

- **Maintain the condition of the inspection vehicle.** The inspector's vehicle should present a professional appearance. Vehicles should be kept clean, with tools and paper supplies neatly organized inside for easy access. Any vehicle problems such as noisy mufflers or squeaky brakes should be fixed immediately.

- **Do *not* smoke or chew tobacco or chew gum during an inspection, do *not* drink on the day of an inspection, and do *not* use illegal drugs.** If you smoke, put out your last cigarette before you leave your vehicle. Do not smoke anywhere on the customer's property— inside or outside. Refrain from drinking during the day and never perform an inspection after having a drink—even if you treat an agent to lunch.

You're not being anti-social. The agent will appreciate your dedication before a scheduled inspection. Save the social hour until inspections are finished for the day.

- **Remember that an inspector is a salesperson.** An inspector's appearance, manner, and performance sells his or her services to the agent and all parties present at an inspection and prepares the way to sell the Home Preservation Plan to previous customers.

- **Do *not* claim to be an Inspection Association member until the association has recognized you as a member.** Inspectors may not misrepresent themselves as being certified by various inspection associations until they pass the exams and receive notification of membership.

INSPECTOR EDUCATION

Training and study courses are provided by the American Home Inspectors Training Institute. Inspectors completing the work are certified by the Institute. Inspector education includes the following:

- Code of ethics and inspector SOPs

- Performance of the home inspection

- Technical instruction in the following:

    —Structural components

    —Exterior, roofing

    —Plumbing system

    —Electrical system

    —Heating system

    —Interiors

    —Insulation, ventilation

    —Environmental issues

    —Sales and marketing

    —Business operations

Ongoing Education

Inspectors are wise to engage in ongoing training in inspection skills. Inspection associations have continuing education requirements for their members, and inspectors must comply with these requirements if they want to renew their membership. The American Home Inspectors Training Institute is approved by many associations to provide training courses for membership renewal credits.

Each home inspector also should improve his or her home inspection skills, remain up to date in new building technologies and home systems, and maintain relevant memberships.

INSPECTION EQUIPMENT

This section of the manual lists inspection tools that are recommended by *AHIT*. Each inspector will need them when performing a successful general inspection using standard visual techniques.

General Items

Following are recommended general supplies for performing an inspection:

- Clean, well-running vehicle

- GPS on IPhone, tablet

- *Property Inspection Report*

- Inspection tags

- Opinion form postcard

- Brochures and business cards

- *Home Maintenance Manual*

- Home Preservation Plan promotional items (if selling this optional product)

- Clipboard, ballpoint pens

- Extra shoes, umbrella, coveralls, knee pads, face mask

- Drop cloth, cleaning cloths, handheld vacuum cleaner

- Reference books kept in car

Inspection Tools

Each inspector also should have the following equipment with him or her during the inspection:

- Combustible gas detector

- Rechargeable flashlight

- Non-invasive moisture meter to check moisture stains

- Voltage sniffer and GFCI tester

- Inspection mirror

- Steel measuring tape

- Laser thermometer

- Screwdriver (flat head and Phillips)

- Ratchet set

- Tool carrying case

- Three-prong circuit tester with two-prong adapter

- 2-foot and 4-foot levels

- Folding ladder (17-foot minimum)

- Binoculars

Each inspector also may want to have the items included in this nice-to-have list:

- Digital camera

- Handheld, digital recorder

- Electrical test screwdriver

- Continuity tester

Inspector Vehicles

At a minimum, you should have a magnetic company sign on the driver and passenger doors of your company vehicle. Many inspectors are opting for vehicle wraps. These are recommended but not required. I never did and owned two successful inspection companies so optional.

Remember that the vehicle at your customer's curb says a great deal about who you are, how prosperous your home inspection company is, and the quality of your services. Whether you like it or not, image counts.

Supplies should be organized and fit neatly inside the vehicle so that you can access them easily. You should develop a system of storing your equipment and paper supplies so that you can find what you need quickly. Some suggestions for a company vehicle are as follows:

- Car that is reliable and gets good mileage

Insist that all of your inspector vehicles present a positive image, that they be clean and in good repair, and that they be big enough to hold the equipment the inspector carries on the job—no beaters, no noisy mufflers, no squeaky brakes, no clouds of exhaust announcing the inspector's arrival. Also, watch be careful with bumper stickers. What may seem fine to an inspector may be offensive to the customer.

One way to ensure that your inspector vehicles represent your company well is to inspect each vehicle on a regular basis as to the image it presents to your customers. You may be surprised that what seemed like an acceptable vehicle six months ago doesn't "fit the bill" anymore.

THE HOME INSPECTION

The home inspection has evolved over several decades to become what it is today. The following four points give the home inspection a broad definition:

1. A home inspection is a thorough *in-depth visual examination* of the structure and operating components of a home—from top to bottom, inside and outside.

2. It is an *analysis* of the present physical condition of that structure and the operating components.

3. The home inspection is a *communication process* in which the inspector and customer discuss the findings during the inspection.

4. The home inspection is a *written report* on the findings of this examination and analysis.

Communication and People Skills

The key here is that the home inspection is a communication process. Perhaps at no other time is the homebuyer as intensely interested in all aspects and details of a home as when that buyer is about to make a purchase. And at no other time are these details so vital to know. The home inspector's responsibility is to educate that buyer and to make sure he or she understands the findings in the inspector's reports. This is done through communication not only in the written report, but also through constant communication during the inspection.

The home inspector must make good use of both communication skills and people skills. There is a difference between the two. A home inspector may be able to talk nonstop about technical issues but not notice that the customer doesn't understand a word he or she is saying. Or the inspector may not be aware that he or she has talked too much and that the customer's eyes are glazing over with boredom. This inspector isn't using people skills. A home inspector needs to be a keen observer of people and be sensitive to what is happening to them.

Here are some communication guidelines to keep in mind when performing home inspections:

1. **Communicate continually during the inspection.** Explain the following for all aspects of the inspection: what you're inspecting, what you're looking or testing for, what you're doing, and what you're finding. For items you're inspecting where the customer is not next to you, such as the roof or crawl space, explain these same points when you've finished.

2. **Let the customer talk and ask questions.** Remember that communication is a two-way street. Don't monopolize the conversation. Let the customer talk too and ask any questions he or she may have. Be patient.

3. **Develop a smooth communication style.** Report good and bad news using the same emotional tone in your voice. Don't be an alarmist. If you find a serious condition, don't say, for example, "Wow! Look at that foundation crack. This whole house is falling apart!" Say, "There's a crack in the foundation, and I'm going to be looking for its cause as we go along." Use a level tone. Likewise, if a condition is not serious, let the customer know. For example, say, "There's a foundation crack, but it appears to have settled some time ago and no longer shows any movement."

4. **Take responsibility for the customer's understanding.** Don't give technical lectures to people with glassy eyes who don't understand what you're talking about. Be sensitive to the customer's attention span. Don't rattle on when the customer isn't listening. Speak in simple terms. There's no need to explain the chemistry of paint; it's enough to explain in simple terms that the paint has broken down and needs to be redone.

5. **Take responsibility for the customer's education.** Sometimes, customers don't really want to listen to an explanation of the findings (for instance, with the electrical system), which they may not understand. But there are important things the customer *must* know for their own safety. The home inspector walks a fine line. You don't want to bore the customer, yet you have a responsibility to inform him or her of important findings. Take that responsibility and be patient. Help the customer to understand what he or she needs to know about the home.

6. **Don't stop talking just because you're inspecting something "simple."** Continue to talk during the inspection even if you're inspecting something as common as a window. Customers still need to hear what you're doing and what you're finding. Sometimes, it's the small tips you give them that they remember best.

7. **Remind the customer of the scope of the inspection.** For your own protection, make sure the customer understands what you're inspecting and what cannot be inspected. This can save you problems and complaints later. For example, the customer should be told that you can't inspect the complete plumbing system because it's partially hidden from view. If the roof is covered with snow and you can't inspect it, you must let the customer know that you cannot report on its condition.

8. **Review the *Property Inspection Report* with the customer after the inspection.** Review the entire report with your customer after the inspection. Even though you've been careful to communicate during the inspection, often the customer will forget some or all of what you've said. Go through the report page by page, including the summary, pointing out where you've indicated certain findings. This review gives you another chance to test the customer's understanding and protects you from complaints later.

CONDUCTING THE HOME INSPECTION

The following pages provide an overview of the home inspection process—from what to do before you leave the office to what to do after you get back.

Preparation

Before leaving the office to keep a scheduled appointment, the inspector should use the following checklist to make sure he or she is prepared for the inspection:

1. Review the appointment sheet for the time of the inspection and the type of inspection to be done.

2. Check that you've got the proper supplies.

3. Check the correct address and use your GPS.

4. Plan the route and travel time.

5. Complete a personal checklist:

   • Clean vehicle

   • Good personal appearance

Before the Customer Arrives

For a buyer inspection, arrive at the property at least 15 minutes early. This gives you time to introduce yourself to the seller before the customer gets there. And it gives you the opportunity to gain general information about the home (the age of the home and the roof, for example). Give the seller a brochure and point out the box noting the structures and components you'll be inspecting.

Use your people skills. The seller may be nervous, worrying that you're going to spoil the sale of the home. Be friendly and reassuring. It may help put the seller at ease by talking about the inspection process. Explain that you'll be careful about tracking in dirt and apologize for the inconvenience. If other family members are present, bring them into the conversation as well.

If it's muddy and wet outside, remember that you'll be walking through the house later. Put on boots and have clean shoes available when you begin the inspection inside. Take a quick look around the exterior of the house, making mental notes. If there's time, walk around the property and fill in as much of the *Property Inspection Report* as you can. But don't disappear. Keep an eye out for the customer's arrival.

Meeting the Customer

When the customer arrives, introduce yourself. Sort out the other people who came along, such as the real estate agent and the friends or family members of the customer. Take some time to talk to each person and give each one a brochure, pointing out the box listing the inspection components as an explanation of what's going to be inspected.

Take the customer aside to discuss the Preinspection Agreement. Privacy is important at this time. The best approach is to go inside and sit at the kitchen table. Have the customer read the agreement, making sure he or she understands the following:

- The definition of an inspection, its content, and its scope, especially what the inspection does not cover.

- The fact that latent or concealed defects are excluded.

- The inspector won't be valuing the property or reporting on compliance with codes or regulations.

- The inspector isn't an insurer or guarantor against defects.

- The inspector doesn't guarantee the fitness, condition, performance, or adequacy of any inspected structure, item, component, or system.

Make sure the customer checks "Yes" or "No" to the statement "Client agrees to release reports to seller/buyer/real estate agent" before he or she signs the agreement.

A WORD OF CAUTION: The home inspection on a typical home should take between two and three hours. An experienced inspector should be able to complete it in two hours without compromising the quality. So although dealing with the Preinspection Agreement is important, an inspector shouldn't spend too much time on it. Each inspector must learn to pace himself or herself.

Having the Customer Present

You may think that a home inspection is strictly a technical job. But as you'll soon learn, being a home inspector also involves a range of interpersonal skills. The number one rule is to have the customer present when you perform the inspection. Communicating your findings as you go along is as important as the inspection itself.

A WORD OF ADVICE: Master the art of conveying your desire to provide the customer with a complete, professional, and meaningful inspection. First, truly *have* the desire to do the best possible job. Second, let the customer know by your words and actions. Show customers your dedication by working hard and intently. Some customers need to see you work physically hard, regardless of your skills and experience. It adds to their level of comfort with the inspection and makes them believe they're getting what they pay for. So let them watch as you walk on the roof, enter the crawl space, and go behind the boiler.

Controlling the Inspection

Depending on the degree of confidentiality the customer has indicated that you keep, the real estate agent may or may not follow along. If the buyer doesn't want the agent to be present, you may have to deal with the situation. Tell the agent that because of the confidentiality clause of the agreement, you are not allowed to complete the inspection in his or her presence. This is not a common situation. Also, it is understood that the seller should not be present during the buyer inspection, but some sellers may try to be there. Again, take the responsibility to have the seller stand aside, doing so in a calm and polite fashion.

Doing the Inspection

In general, conduct the inspection in the order provided in the *Property Inspection Report*—line by line. If you've had the opportunity to fill in some of the exterior information before the customer arrived, retrace your tracks and explain what you've already inspected and recorded. Then continue on. Remember to attach inspection tags in the appropriate places.

Fill out your *Property Inspection Report* as you go along. Don't rely on your memory to fill it in later. Write a clear, concise report, one that can be read and understood easily. The order of the inspection is as follows:

- Grounds

- Roof covering, chimney, gutters

- Siding, trim, windows, doors

- Exterior electrical, A/C compressor (depending on the part of the country you live in. In the south the electrical panels are on the exterior so that is done earlier in the inspection).

- Garage

- General interior

- Kitchen and bathrooms

- Bedrooms and interior windows

- Fireplaces

- Attic

- Basement, crawl space

- Plumbing and electrical

- Heating, cooling systems

Reviewing the Report

When the inspection is completed, sit down with the customer to conclude your business. The kitchen table, out of the way of other parties, is a good place for this conference.

Fill in any additional comments and summary items on the last pages of the *Property Inspection Report*. Then page through the report with the customer. Remind him or her of the significant findings you mentioned during the inspection and answer any questions.

Encourage the customer to read the report thoroughly sometime later as an important reminder what you discussed. This is particularly important with regard to liability issues. Many customers forget what the inspection findings were and do not read the report. These are the people you may hear from later with complaints.

Finishing the Job

After reviewing the report, collect the inspection fee and check the receipt box on your digital report (85% of inspectors use a digital report). Fees are to be paid at the inspection site. Don't back down on this point. If a customer has forgotten his or her checkbook, be helpful. Some inspectors have been very creative—even going with customers to an automatic teller machine while they withdraw cash. Perhaps consider using a service such as Square that allows you to charge credit cards via an iPad or IPhone.

Back at the Office

After each inspection, the inspector must complete the tasks that follow. More information about the office aspects of the inspection is presented in *THE OFFICE PLAN*.

1. Always complete a Post-Inspection Form. It serves as a reminder of follow-up actions that need to be taken, such as:

   • Enter all relevant pick-up appointments.

   • Send a follow-up letter for a potential review inspection.

   • Send follow-up letters to the customer, real estate agent, and/or seller.

   • Send thank-you card to the customer, real estate agent, and/or seller.

   • Invoice the customer (in rare circumstances when the fee was not collected).

   • Return to the site (in special instances when something couldn't be inspected).

   • Send letter for the customer (when the customer's lender or another party has requested a letter confirming inspection findings).

   • Send report copy to customer(s).

   • Make additional comments.

2. Include a Post-Inspection Form and the appointment sheet along with the copy of the *Property Inspection Report.*

3. Clip the check to the front of the paperwork.

4. Process all checks and follow-up information as outlined in the office plan.

UNDERSTANDING LIABILITY

Every inspector should understand that liability concerns rank as a number one issue in the home inspection industry. Twenty-five years ago might have been a time of "buyer beware." But today, with the rise of consumerism, the buyer is more likely to sue if something goes wrong or if the buyer suspects that something is wrong.

Prevention

AHIT takes a proactive approach to liability, that is, a plan of aggressive prevention. Inspectors need to follow the steps below to avoid the complaints and lawsuits that are rife in the home inspection business. (Insurance and complaint handling are more fully discussed in *THE OFFICE PLAN*.) For liability measures, the inspector will:

- **Carefully review the PreInspection Agreement with the customer and obtain the customer's signature.** Some customers freeze when they are asked to read and sign the Preinspection Agreement. Be patient and helpful. Offer to review each clause of the agreement with the customer. Make sure the customer understands the agreement.

- **Perform a quality inspection.** The inspector must have mastered the technical and analytical skills necessary to perform good inspections. Each inspector must do an excellent job in inspecting a home and in complying with the SOPs of his or her inspection association.

- **Ask the customer to be present throughout the inspection and explain what you are doing and what you have discovered.** Here, your interpersonal skills come into play. Make sure the customer understands what structure or component you are testing, what you are looking for, and what defects and deficiencies you have found. Of course, your liability is highest when the customer isn't present at the inspection.

- **Write a clear, precise report and review the report with the customer.** Report accurately. Don't take shortcuts with the *Property Inspection Report*. After the inspection is over, sit down with the customer and go through the report, reminding him or her of any significant defects or deficiencies you found during the inspection.

- **Encourage customers to read the Property Inspection Report after you leave.** Some customers never read the report and forget what the inspection revealed. These are often the customers who complain or threaten legal action later.